First Edition

biography for beginners

African-American Leaders, Volume 1

Civil Rights, Political, and Social Leaders; Scientists and Inventors; and Athletes

Laurie Lanzen Harris,
Editor

Favorable Impressions

P.O. Box 69018 • Pleasant Ridge, MI 48069

Laurie Lanzen Harris, *Editor*
Frank R. Abate, PhD; Laurie Collier Hillstrom,
Claire A. Rewold, PhD, *Contributing Editors*
Dan R. Harris, *Senior Vice President, Sales and Marketing*

Library of Congress Cataloging-in-Publication Data

Biography for beginners : African-American leaders / Laurie Lanzen Harris, editor.
    p. cm.
  Includes bibliographical references and index.
  ISBN 978-1-931360-35-7 (alk. paper)
  1. African Americans—Biography—Dictionaries, Juvenile. 2. Successful people—United States—Biography—Dictionaries, Juvenile. 3. African American leadership—Dictionaries, Juvenile. I. Harris, Laurie Lanzen. II. Title: African-American Leaders.
  E185.96.B475 2007
  902'.009296073—dc22
  [B]   2007041045

ISBN 1-931360-35-9
ISBN-13 978-1-931360-35-7

The information in this publication was compiled from the sources cited and from other sources considered reliable. While every possible effort has been made to ensure reliability, the publisher will not assume liability for damages caused by inaccuracies in the data, and makes no warranty, express or implied, on the accuracy of the information contained herein.

This book is printed on acid-free paper meeting the ANSI Z39.48 Standard. The infinity symbol that appears above indicate that the paper in this book meets that standard.

Printed in the United States

Contents

Preface

Welcome to *Biography for Beginners: African-American Leaders, Volume 1*. This is the first of a two-volume series and covers civil rights, political, and social leaders; scientists and inventors; and athletes. Volume Two in the series will feature profiles of African-American actors, artists, authors, dancers, musicians, and entrepreneurs.

Since beginning the *Biography for Beginners* series in 1995, we have published four monographs in areas of high interest for young readers, including U.S. Presidents, world explorers, authors, and inventors. Three years ago we surveyed librarians for additional areas of interest for young readers, and they suggested African-American leaders.

The Plan of the Work

Like *Biography for Beginners: Presidents of the United States, World Explorers*, and *Inventors, African-American Leaders* is written for early readers, ages 7 to 10. The volume is especially created for young students in a format they can read, understand, and use for assignments. The 37 entries are arranged alphabetically. Each entry begins with a heading listing the individual's name, birth and death dates, and a brief description of his or her importance to the history of African-American achievement. Boldfaced headings lead readers to information on birth, youth, growing up, education, marriage and family, and the nature of the individual's accomplishment.

Entries end with a list of World Wide Web sites. These sites have been reviewed for accuracy and suitability for use by young students. A bibliography of works used in the compilation of the entries is at the end of the Preface.

The entries also include portraits of the individual, as well as paintings, photos, and other illustrations to enhance the reader's understanding of the person's achievement.

Audience

This book is intended for young readers in grades two through five who are studying African-American history for the first time. Most children will use this book to study one individual at a time, usually as part of a class assignment. Within the entries, the names of other individuals who appear in the volume are bold-faced, to act as a cross-reference. A Glossary of terms common to Black American history appears at the end of the book. This section also contains brief biographies of people important to African-American history. The Glossary terms appear in the text in bold-faced capitals.

Index

An Index covering names, occupations, and key words concludes the volume. The Index has been created with the young reader in mind, and therefore contains a limited number of terms that have been simplified for ease of research.

Our Advisors

Biography for Beginners: African-American Leaders was reviewed by an Advisory Board that includes school librarians and public librarians. The thoughtful comments and suggestions of all the Board members have been invaluable in developing this publication. Any errors, however, are mine alone. I would like to list the members of the Advisory Board and to thank them again for their efforts.

Linda Carpino	Detroit Public Library Detroit, MI
Nina Levine	Blue Mountain Middle School Cortlandt Manor, NY
Nancy Margolin	McDougle Elementary School Chapel Hill, NC
Deb Rothaug	Pasadena Elementary School Plainview, NY
Laurie Scott	Farmington Hills Community Library Farmington Hills, MI
Joyce Siler	Westridge Elementary School Kansas City, MO

Your Comments Are Welcome

Our goal is to provide accurate, accessible biographical information for early readers. Please write or call me with your comments.

Acknowledgments

I would like to thank the staffs of the many organizations who provided photos and illustrations for the volume, as well as the Library of Congress. Thank you to Sans Serif for outstanding design and layout.

Bibliography

This is a listing of works used in the compilation of the biographical profiles. Most of the works cited here are written at the middle school or high school reading level and are generally beyond the reading level of early elementary students. However, many librarians consider these reliable, objective points of departure for further research.

Ashe, Arthur. *A Hard Road to Glory,* 1993.
Columbia Encyclopedia, 2005 ed.
Compton's Encyclopedia, 2005 ed.
Daley, James, ed. *Great Speeches by African Americans*, Dover Publications, 2006.
Douglass, Frederick. *Narrative of the Life of Frederick Douglass, An American Slave,* 1845.

Laurie Harris, Editor and Publisher
Favorable Impressions

Introduction

The men and women profiled in this volume have distinguished themselves in many areas of achievement: in politics, social activism, science, invention, and sports. What unites them is their African-American heritage, a heritage that includes the brutal history of slavery, racism, and the fight for equality and freedom. It is not the purpose of this volume to simply outline the struggles faced by these individuals. Rather, it is to celebrate their achievements, and to show how they confronted ignorance and bigotry to bring about change in each of their areas of accomplishment. Their methods were as different as their areas of achievement, whether in politics, science, or sports. Yet there is one characteristic that unites them all, and that is their courage. Time after time, these stories reveal the strength and perseverance of these men and women as they confronted the shameful bigotry that would deny them their rights based upon their racial heritage.

Civil Rights, Political, and Social Leaders

The ideal of freedom and equality motivated many of the individuals profiled here to work for abolition, Civil Rights, and other movements for social and political change. The earliest entry is on **Crispus Attucks**, a former slave who lost his life in the Boston Massacre. Next, we reach the era of the great abolitionists. **Frederick Douglass** escaped slavery and became the most powerful writer and orator in the cause of abolition. After the Civil War, he worked tirelessly to ensure the passage of constitutional amendments to guarantee former slaves their hard-won freedoms. **Sojourner Truth** was also a powerful speaker for abolition and women's rights. **Harriet Tubman** was the greatest of the Conductors of the Underground Railroad, leading hundreds of slaves to freedom, and serving as a spy and nurse for the Union during the Civil War.

W.E.B. Du Bois was a distinguished historian and early leader in the fight for Civil Rights. He broke with some African-American leaders, including **Booker T. Washington**, over the methods and goals of the movement for equality. Washington devoted his life to educating African-American students, and founded the Tuskegee Institute. **Mary McLeod Bethune** was tireless in reaching her goals of creating an outstanding school for African-Americans, and worked for integration in many areas, including the military and the Red Cross.

Ida B. Wells was a fearless journalist who risked great personal danger to expose the brutal reality of lynching to the American public. **Ralph Bunche** fought for Civil Rights at home, as a founding member of the NAACP, and abroad as a member of the United Nations. He was the first person of color to receive the Nobel Prize for Peace.

With **Thurgood Marshall**, we come to an individual whose achievements truly defined the Civil Rights Movement of the 20th century. Marshall was the lead lawyer for the NAACP. He argued, and won, the landmark Civil Rights case of the era, Brown vs. the Board of Education. Later, after a distinguished career as both a lawyer and a jurist, he was the first African-American to serve on the Supreme Court.

Martin Luther King Jr. is a man whose name is synonymous with the struggle for Civil Rights. As an author, speaker, organizer, and activist, he outlined the goals and methods of the movement, fighting social injustice in a way that revealed to the world the evil of bigotry, and the dignity of those who sought racial equality. He helped choose the arrest of **Rosa Parks** to rally the movement around the Montgomery Bus Boycott, one of the most important protests of the era. **Coretta Scott King** worked closely with her husband and continued his work for social justice after his assassination. **Jesse Jackson** was an early and ardent follower of King. Jackson continues to be an activist in the fight for racial equality.

Malcolm X was a galvanizing figure. He rejected the methods and goals of the Civil Rights movement, championing instead the separatist philosophy of the Nation of Islam. Over the years his thinking evolved on racial equality and social justice, but his life, too, was cut short by assassination.

Colin Powell broke many racial barriers in his distinguished military and political career. He was the first African-American to become a four-star general in the Army, and the first African-American Secretary of State. **Condoleezza Rice** broke many barriers as well. She was the first African-American woman to serve as Provost of Stanford University, the first woman to serve as National Security Advisor, and the first African-American woman to become Secretary of State.

Leaders in the Areas of Science and Invention

Benjamin Banneker was an astronomer, inventor, and mathematician and is considered the first African-American scientist. **Elijah McCoy** invented the automatic lubricating oil cup, defending his patents from those who thought an African-American was incapable of his scientific advances. **George Washington Carver** faced discrimination in schooling and work, yet overcame those obstacles to invent more than 300 products, and to become an important educator at Washington's Tuskegee Institute. **Matthew Henson** was Robert Peary's most important colleague in his explorations of the Arctic and North Pole. **Garrett Morgan**, like McCoy, faced discrimination from those who thought a black man could never have invented the gas mask and the traffic signal. These life-saving devices, still in use today, are a testament to his science and his perseverance. **Ben Carson**, one of the finest pediatric neurosurgeons of his generation, makes a point of speaking to African-American students about the importance of science and school. **Lonnie Johnson**, a NASA scientist, invented the SuperSoaker, and also speaks to children about science and scientific careers. **Mae Jemison**, the first African-American woman astronaut, continues to do research and encourage young African-Americans to get involved in science.

Sports

One of the greatest baseball pitchers of all time, **Satchel Paige**, was forced to play in the Negro Leagues for years. Only after the legendary **Jackie Robinson** broke the "color line" in 1946 did professional sports open up for African-Americans. Robinson endured years of racial insults, but he proved to the world that the worth of an athlete had nothing to do with color. He paved the way for generations of African-American players in every sport. But racism hadn't yet left the major leagues. When **Hank Aaron** drew close to the home run record held by Babe Ruth, he received death threats from those who didn't want a black man to break it. He persevered, and went on to one of the greatest careers in baseball history.

Three African-American track athletes who became legends of the sport were **Jesse Owens, Wilma Rudolph,** and **Jackie Joyner-Kersee.** Jesse Owens won a record four gold medals at the 1936 Olympics, revealing the lie at the heart of the racial supremacy promoted by Adolf Hitler and the Nazis. Wilma Rudolph overcame polio and prejudice to win three gold medals at the Olympics of 1956. Jackie Joyner-Kersee is considered by many to be the finest female athlete of the 20th century, a title she earned by winning a total of six Olympic medals over the course of her career.

Muhammad Ali is also an Olympic gold medalist, and the only person to win the heavyweight boxing title three times. An outspoken advocate for social justice, he continues to inspire people today. **Bill Russell**, one of the finest players ever to play the game of basketball, was the first African-American to coach an NBA team, and the first to be elected to the Hall of Fame. **Michael Jordan** is now considered the finest basketball player of all time, and a leader in the business and charity world, too. **Jim Brown** had one of the greatest football careers in NFL history, and is considered by many the finest running back to ever play the game. Today he heads organizations to help disadvantaged African-Americans.

Arthur Ashe was born into a world where African-Americans couldn't play on the same tennis courts, or even the same tennis leagues, as their white counterparts. His career is full of record-breaking firsts. He was the first African-American to win the U.S. National men's singles title, the U.S. Open, and to be ranked #1 in the world. He was also a tireless advocate for social justice around the world, whether against apartheid in South Africa, or for patients with AIDS.

Tiger Woods, the youngest person in this volume, is in the midst of one of the greatest professional golf careers in history, and is considered the most accomplished player of any racial background ever to play the sport.

It is perhaps a testament to the power of social change that this young man has achieved the highest level of play in his sport, as well as the accolades of the sports world, without facing the racial barriers confronted by earlier athletes profiled here. Outspoken and proud of his ethnic heritage as an African-American and Asian-American, Woods, too, devotes his time and talents to helping young people achieve in school and in sport.

Hank Aaron
1934 -
African-American Professional Baseball Player
All-Time Career Leader in RBIs, Second in Home Runs

HANK AARON WAS BORN on February 5, 1934, in Mobile, Alabama. His full name is Henry Louis Aaron. He was the third of eight children born to Herbert and Estella Aaron. The family lived in a poor neighborhood of Mobile called Down the Bay, a predominately black neighborhood.

The mid-1930s was the time of the Great Depression in America, with millions struggling in poverty. Herbert Aaron supported his large family as a dockworker near Mobile Bay. The family later moved to Toulminville, on the outskirts of Mobile.

HANK AARON GREW UP loving to play sports. He played stickball as many children did then, using broomsticks as bats. When he was 14, his father took him to see the Brooklyn Dodgers play. Hank saw **Jackie Robinson**, the first African-American in Major League Baseball. He also attended a speech Robinson gave after the game. It inspired him to try to make it in baseball.

HANK AARON WENT TO SCHOOL at the local public schools. He attended Central High School, then Josephine Allen Institute. He was a star football player, but neither school had a baseball team. Still, Hank's athletic talent got him noticed by area baseball teams. When he was a junior in high school, he started playing semiprofessional baseball for the Mobile Black Bears. He was paid ten dollars a game.

PLAYING IN THE NEGRO LEAGUES: Aaron's talent got the attention of Ed Scott, a scout for the Indianapolis Clowns of the Negro League. Although Major League Baseball had signed a few black ballplayers, there were still all-black professional teams. So Aaron began playing in the Negro League in 1952. At the age of 18, he led the league in batting with an average of .467, despite using an unconventional cross-handed grip.

Midway through the 1952 season, the Boston Braves of the National League purchased Aaron's contract. They assigned him to their minor league team in Eau Claire, Wisconsin. There he was switched from shortstop to outfield, and his cross-handed grip was corrected to a conventional batting style.

Hank Aaron hits his 600th major league home run
in Atlanta, April 28, 1971.

FACING RACISM: The next season Aaron moved up to the Braves minor league team in Florida, the Jacksonville Tars of the South Atlantic League. As one of the only black players on a team playing in the South, Aaron played amid open racial hatred. When he traveled with his team, he was forced to eat in separate facilities for "Coloreds Only" and live in segregated hotels. This was a time in America of **JIM CROW**, with racial discrimination not only common but written into law. Still, Aaron played very well, batting .362, and winning the Most Valuable Player award in the league for 1953.

STARTING IN THE MAJOR LEAGUES: Aaron started in the major leagues because of an injury to one of the Braves's starters, Bobby Thomson. Thomson broke his ankle in spring training in 1954, and Aaron was called up to play outfield.

By this time the Braves had moved from Boston to Milwaukee. Aaron would stay with the Braves organization as a player for the next 21 seasons. In 1955 he switched to right field. He was a great fielder, and during his Major League career he won three Gold Glove awards. (The Gold Glove honors the top player at his position in the league.)

But it was Aaron's power as a hitter that made him a star. He was a consistent slugger with good power in his early career. He hit over .300 consistently, and hit at least 20 home runs over 20 consecutive seasons, from 1955 through 1974.

In 1957 Aaron led the Milwaukee Braves to the National League pennant. In the 1957 World Series, the Braves upset the favored New York Yankees, with Aaron leading his team to the championship. In the Series, Aaron hit three home runs and batted .393. He won the National League Most Valuable Player award that season.

In 1958 the Braves again won the National League pennant, led by Aaron and Red Schoendienst. Aaron batted .326 for the regular

*Aaron breaks Babe Ruth's record for career home runs
as he hits no. 715 on April 8, 1974.*

season, with 34 home runs, and hit .333 in the World Series. But this time the Braves lost to the Yankees in the World Series.

"HAMMERIN' HANK": Aaron earned the nickname "Hammerin' Hank" over his long career of consistent hitting. "I looked for one pitch my whole career, a breaking ball," he told the New York *Daily News*. "I never worried about the fastball. They couldn't throw it by me, none of them."

The pitchers agreed. "Trying to throw a fastball by Henry Aaron is like trying to sneak a sunrise past a rooster," lamented Curt Simmons.

After hitting three home runs in a single game in 1959, Aaron was paid $30,000 to appear in a TV show called "Home Run Derby." On that show, power hitters faced off against batting practice pitching to see who could hit the most home runs. After earning almost as much as his annual salary in one show, Aaron decided to alter his batting style to increase his power hitting. As he told *Sporting News*, "I noticed that they never had a show called 'Singles Derby.'"

Through the 1960s the Braves had mostly winning seasons, but no pennants. In 1966 the Braves moved to Atlanta, becoming the first Major League team based in the Deep South. As Aaron's career lengthened, he started to move up on the list in several all-time career statistics. His durability and consistency were paying off. By 1972 he was the highest paid player in the league, with a salary of $200,000. And he was approaching the "unbreakable" all-time career home run record of Babe Ruth.

FACING A RACIST BACKLASH: As he neared the record of the still much-loved Babe Ruth, Aaron felt the sting of racism again. In the early 1970s, he received up to 3,000 letters a day as he neared Ruth's record of 714 career home runs. Many of the letters were filled with racial slurs and even death threats. But there were also many fans who supported Aaron, such as one who wrote, "Dear Mr. Aaron, I am twelve years old, and I wanted to tell you that I have read many articles about the prejudice against you. I really think it is bad. I don't care what color you are."

Hank Aaron quietly went about his business. He recalls that he really didn't feel the pressure. "I never felt pressured because I felt the only way I could play baseball was to relax and do the

Aaron at his induction into the Alabama Academy of Honor, August 20, 2007.

best I could. I couldn't play under pressure."

By the end of the 1973 season Aaron had 713 home runs. On Opening Day, April 4, 1974, Aaron tied Ruth's record with a home run at Cincinnati. The Braves returned home to play the Los Angeles Dodgers next. On April 8, off pitcher Al Downing, Hank Aaron hit career home run 715, surpassing the record Ruth had set in 1935.

Aaron was now 40 years old, and nearing the end of his career. At the end of the 1974 season he was traded to the Milwaukee Brewers, and so finished his career with two seasons in the American League. He went on to hit an all-time career high of 755 home runs. That record stood until 2007, when it was broken by Barry Bonds.

Aaron retired in 1976 with a career batting average of .305. His 2,297 runs batted in is the all-time record, and he has the third highest total hits, 3,771, behind only Pete Rose and Ty Cobb.

HANK AARON'S HOME AND FAMILY: Aaron has been married twice. His first wife was named Barbara Lucas. They married in

1953 and divorced in 1971. In 1971 he married Billye Williams. The couple have raised five children and have several grand-children.

HIS LEGACY: Hank Aaron earned the respect of America not only with his play, but with his modesty, consistency, and courage. After his baseball career ended he was hired by the Atlanta Braves front office to help acquire new talent. With his help the Braves went on to become one of the most successful teams of the 1990s. Aaron also worked for Turner Broadcasting and CNN. He has been successful in his own businesses in the Atlanta area, and has been active in fund-raising and charities.

On the 25th anniversary of his record-breaking home run, Major League Baseball created the Hank Aaron Award. It honors the top players in the National and American Leagues who combine five offensive abilities: home runs, RBIs, stolen bases, runs scored, and batting average. It's a fitting tribute to a man who was one of the finest players the game has ever seen.

WORLD WIDE WEB SITES:

http://www.baseballhalloffame.prg/hofers/detail.jsp?playerid=11001
http://www.sportingnews.com/archives/aaron/
http://sports.espn.go.com/mlb/

Muhammad Ali
1942 -
African-American Boxer and
Three-time Heavyweight Champion

MUHAMMAD ALI WAS BORN on January 18, 1942, in Louisville, Kentucky. His name when he was born was Cassius Marcellus Clay Jr. He took the name Muhammad Ali when he converted to the Nation of Islam faith as an adult.

His parents were Cassius and Odessa Clay. Cassius was a sign painter and Odessa was a housekeeper. He had a brother named Rudolph.

MUHAMMAD ALI GREW UP in a poor but loving household. He remembers that while they had enough to eat, there was little left for anything else. "We never owned a car that was less than ten years old. The rain was coming in through the roof and walls. Most of the clothes we got came from the Good Will."

Despite the lack of money, the family was close. His father loved to sing and dance. His mother brought up her sons to value family and faith. They went to church every Sunday. "She taught us to love people and treat everybody with kindness," he recalled. To help out at home, Ali took a job as a janitor at a local college.

Ali also grew up at a time when African-Americans were denied equal rights. It was the time of **JIM CROW** laws. "In those days most of the restaurants, hotels, and movies in Louisville, as in all of the South, were either closed to blacks or had segregated sections," said Ali. He grew up during the movement for **CIVIL RIGHTS**. He would take a special place in it.

STARTING TO BOX: The story of how Ali came to boxing has become a legend. He'd ridden his new bicycle to Louisville's Columbia Auditorium. While he was inside, his bike was stolen. He was told to report the theft to a policeman named Joe Martin, who was teaching boxing in the auditorium's basement.

When Ali got inside the gym, his life changed. "The sights and sounds and the smell of the boxing gym excited me so much that I almost forgot about the bike." From that day forward, he couldn't get enough of boxing. He couldn't even wait to learn how to box.

"I was so eager I jumped into the ring with some older boxer and began throwing wild punches. In a minute my nose started bleeding. My mouth was hurt. My head was dizzy. Finally someone pulled me out of the ring."

He loved the sport. And he felt as if God had intended him to follow the path of boxing to greatness. "I always felt like I was born to do something for my people. Then my bike got stolen and I started boxing. It was like God telling me that boxing was my responsibility."

Soon, Ali was boxing in televised amateur matches. He got four dollars per match. As he grew older and developed even greater skills, he started to win local, state, and national championships.

MUHAMMAD ALI WENT TO SCHOOL at the local public schools in Louisville. He didn't do particularly well in school, because all he could think about was boxing. He graduated from Central High School in Louisville in 1960. That same year, he became an international star.

THE 1960 OLYMPICS: Ali went to the 1960 Olympics after establishing himself as one of the best boxers in the nation. By the age of 18, he'd won 100 out of 108 fights. He'd won two Golden Gloves titles, an important national competition. He'd also won two competitions sponsored by the AAU (Amateur Athletic Association). It's important to remember that until the 1990s, no pro athletes could compete in the Olympics. It existed to promote the values of amateur athletics.

Ali's boxing skill, and his outgoing personality, made him a favorite at the Olympics, played in Rome that year. He won all his

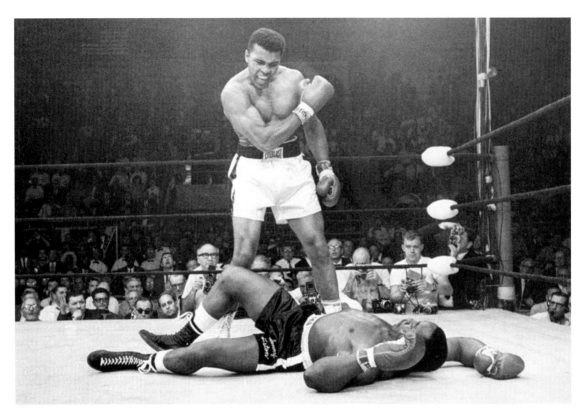

Ali knocks down Sonny Liston to defend his heavyweight title, May 25, 1965.

matches, including the final gold medal round. In that match, he beat a rival from Poland to take home the medal for America.

Back in Louisville, Ali was greeted by fans, both black and white. But when the Olympic hero and his brother tried to eat at a Louisville restaurant, they were refused service because they were black. Ali was furious. He tossed his gold medal into the nearby Ohio River.

GOING PRO: Ali decided to turn pro after the Olympics. He was tired of being poor. He wanted to finally make money from the sport he loved. The clothes he had were worn and torn. His shoes had holes in them. "I had never been able to afford a first-class mouthpiece to protect my teeth. I had to wait until other fighters finished so I could borrow their headgear, or their trunks, or bandages."

A group of wealthy white men from Louisville became Ali's sponsors. They paid him $10,000, and they received the rights to one-half of the money he made over six years.

Soon, Ali was fighting pro matches as a heavyweight. (Boxing is divided into classifications by weight. At that time, heavyweight boxers weighed 175 pounds or more.) He got off to a great start in the fall of 1960, winning his first 19 matches. He was known to fans for his incredible quickness, weaving to avoid a punch, then landing one on his opponent. He was also known for his colorful personality. Long before rap, he would make up witty rhymes about his opponents on the spot.

HEAVYWEIGHT CHAMPIONSHIP: In 1964, after four years of hard work, training, and winning matches, Ali was ready to take his shot at the championship. He faced Sonny Liston, the reigning champion. He was ready. He'd studied Liston's style, and he knew his weaknesses. He also knew how to get inside Liston's head. "I figured Liston would get so mad that he'd try to kill me and forget everything he knew about boxing."

And that's pretty much what happened. Ali taunted Liston in the days leading up to the fight. When they got in the ring, Liston's anger overcame his training. He swung without landing punches. Ali had been right. Through speed and skill, he bested Liston. He became the heavyweight champion of the world.

"I am the greatest!" Ali claimed. He had predicted, and achieved, "a total eclipse of the Sonny."

Ali in his title bout against George Foreman,
October, 1974, in Kinshasa, Zaire.

JOINING THE NATION OF ISLAM: The day after winning the heavy-weight championship, Ali made an announcement. He was joining the Nation of Islam. And he was changing his name from Cassius Clay to Muhammad Ali. "Clay was my slave name," he declared. He wanted to be identified with a new name and a new faith.

The brash, outspoken Ali took the sports world by surprise. Most Americans knew little about the Nation of Islam, or the Black Muslims as they are also called. Ali didn't care what others thought. "I don't have to be what you want me to be," he said. "I'm free to be what I want." Not caring about the controversy, Ali went on to win his next nine fights.

REFUSING TO GO INTO THE ARMY: In 1967, Ali was back in the headlines, but not for his boxing. He had been drafted into the Army, and he refused to serve. At that time, the U.S. was involved in the Vietnam War. Some Americans were beginning to question why the U.S. was fighting in Vietnam. Ali, always outspoken, was one of them. "I ain't got no quarrel with them Viet Cong," he said. (The Viet Cong was the name of the North Vietnamese army. They were Communists, and supported by the Soviet Union. The South Vietnamese were supported by the U.S.)

Ali applied to be a "conscientious objector." That's someone whose beliefs prevent them from fighting in a war. His application was denied. Still he refused to join the Army. It was an action that was against the law.

His resistance was based on his faith and on his view of the treatment of African-Americans. "Why should they ask me to put on a uniform and go 10,000 miles from home and drop bombs and bullets on brown people in Vietnam while so-called Negro people in Louisville are treated like dogs? If I thought going to war would bring freedom and equality to 22 million of my people, they wouldn't have to draft me. I'd join tomorrow."

Ali was found guilty of breaking the draft laws. He was sentenced to five years in jail, and fined $10,000. He appealed the decision and remained free while his appeal made its way through the court system.

BOXING TITLE TAKEN AWAY: The World Boxing Association took away Ali's heavyweight championship title. They also took away his boxing license, so he wasn't able to make a living as a boxer.

For the next three years, Ali spoke out against the war. He became more involved in the struggle for Civil Rights. And his case made it's way to the Supreme Court.

REVERSAL OF HIS CONVICTION: In June 1970, the U.S. Supreme Court ruled that the government had acted improperly in handling Ali's case. They reversed his conviction. He was free to make his living as a boxer again.

Ali decided to contact Joe Frazier, then the heavyweight champion, to get ready for a chance to win back his title. "This might shock and amaze ya, but I'm going to retire Joe Frazier," he predicted. He and Frazier fought in March 1971 at Madison Square Garden. It was a long and brutal battle—both fighters wound up in the hospital afterward. When it was over, Frazier had won.

Soon, Ali was ready to fight again. He fought a number of matches in preparation for another shot at his old title. That finally happened in October, 1974.

HEAVYWEIGHT CHAMPION AGAIN: Ali fought George Foreman, then the reigning champ, for the heavyweight crown in Kinshasa, Zaire. Ali was ready. He knocked Foreman out in eight rounds, in a fight that became known as "the rumble in the jungle." Once again, he was heavyweight champion of the world.

Ali fought 10 title matches to hold on to the boxing championship. He was the only person ever to win the heavyweight title three times. But he was getting older. The wear and tear of boxing was beginning to show. He first announced that he would retire in 1979. He came back to the game briefly, but retired for good in 1981. He ended his career with an incredible record of 56-5.

PARKINSON'S DISEASE: In the late 1970s, Ali's doctors began to notice that he was having health problems. He had trouble walking and talking. His hands shook and he was weak. He was tested and was found to have Parkinson's disease. That's a disease of the neurological system and affects the brain's ability to control movement and speech. His doctors believe that years of taking powerful blows to the head led to brain damage, and to his current disability.

Ali refused to be bitter about his physical state. He started a new career, raising money for Parkinson's research and many other charities.

AN OLYMPIC SYMBOL AGAIN: In 1996, Ali carried the torch into Olympic Stadium in Atlanta, Georgia. He lit the Olympic Flame to begin the 1996 Games. He was seen by billions of viewers all over the world. They saw a former athletic champion diminished by disease, but still a star.

AMBASSADOR TO THE WORLD: Despite his physical problems, Ali remains an active member of the international community. He travels the world bringing food and medicine to people in need. He has met with world leaders to promote peace. He is one of the best-known and most-beloved athletes in history.

*Muhammad Ali poses for cameras
while visiting Detroit, Michigan, January 17, 2007.*

In 2005, Ali opened the Muhammad Ali Center. It's an international cultural and educational center. Devoted to promoting Ali's values and ideals, its mission is "to promote respect, hope, and understanding, and to inspire adults and children everywhere to be as great as they can be."

MUHAMMAD ALI'S HOME AND FAMILY: Ali has been married four times. He and his first wife, Sonji Roi, were married from 1964 to 1966. His second wife was Belinda Boyd. They married in 1967 and had four children: Maryum, Rasheeda, Famillah, and Muhammad Jr. They divorced in 1976. Ali's third wife was Veronica Porche.

They were married from 1977 to 1986. They had two daughters, Hana and Laila. Laila is now a boxer herself. Ali married Lonnie Williams in 1986. They have an adopted son, Asaad. Ali also has two daughters, Khalia and Miya, with two other women.

Ali and Lonnie bought a house in Louisville in 2007. They also have homes in Arizona and Michigan.

HIS LEGACY: In the opinion of most observers, Ali is the greatest boxer of all time, and one of the finest athletes of the 20th century. **Hank Aaron** summed up his legacy.

"I don't think there will ever be another fighter like Muhammad Ali. For a guy to be that big and move the way he did. It was like music, poetry, no question about it. And for what he did outside the ring, Ali will always be remembered. Children in this country should be taught forever how he stood by his convictions and led his life. He's someone that black people, white people, people all across the country whatever their color, can be proud of."

WORLD WIDE WEB SITES:

http://www.alicenter.org
http://www.ali.com/greatest
http://www.time.com/time/time100/heroes/prfile/ali01.html

Arthur Ashe

1943 - 1993
African-American Professional Tennis Player, Author, and Activist
First African-American to Achieve #1 Ranking in Pro Tennis

ARTHUR ASHE WAS BORN on July 10, 1943, in Richmond, Virginia. His full name was Arthur Ashe Jr. His parents were Arthur Ashe Sr. and Mattie Ashe. Arthur Sr. was a superintendent in Richmond's recreation department. His mother was a homemaker. Arthur had a younger brother, John.

Tragically, Mattie Ashe died when Arthur was six. He and his brother were raised by their father and a housekeeper, Mrs. Otis

Berry. Ashe's father married Lorene Kimbrough when Arthur was 12. The family grew to include a stepsister, Loretta, and a stepbrother, Robert.

ARTHUR ASHE GREW UP in a loving, nurturing family. Perhaps the most important influence on Ashe throughout his life was his father. He taught Arthur the importance of hard work, discipline, and respect. Throughout his career in tennis, Ashe was known for his professional, polite ways. He learned that from his father, too. "You don't get nowhere by making enemies," his father told him. "You gain by helping others. Things that you need come first. Foolishness is last."

TENNIS AND RACIAL EQUALITY: There are two major themes in the life of Arthur Ashe. One is tennis. The other is the struggle for racial equality. Ashe was able to trace his ancestry back to his great grandparents. They had all been slaves. The legacy of racism reached back into his family's history. He was determined to fight it in his own time, and in his own way.

Ashe grew up in the black section of Richmond. At that time, Virginia, and much of the South, was segregated. That meant that separate facilities, from buses to tennis courts, severely limited the lives of black people.

ARTHUR ASHE WENT TO SCHOOL at all-black schools in Richmond. He attended Baker Elementary in Richmond, where he was a great student. He also remembered the way that black students were made to feel about themselves. He recalled, "the unmistakable impression left in black school children that there is not much they can do beyond being garbage men or mailmen. You might be a policeman, but never a bank president, mayor, or chief of police. Every black kid I knew grew up feeling that certain jobs were off-limits. Books and the Pledge of Allegiance said one thing, but once you left school, you had to live in a completely different set of circumstances."

STARTING TO PLAY TENNIS: Ashe started to play tennis at the age of six. He played on the courts at Richmond's Brook Field. He'd watch white kids playing at Byrd Park, where it was illegal for blacks to play.

While playing on Brook Field, Ashe got noticed. Ronald Charity, a local teacher, saw him play and recognized his talent. He became his first coach. Soon Arthur was entering tournaments.

Ashe's next coach was a man named Dr. Robert Walter Johnson. Johnson had a mission: to help black players break into the world of tennis, then a world of rich, white players.

At that time, blacks weren't allowed to play in the all-white USLTA (U.S. Lawn Tennis Association). Instead, they played in their own league, the ATA (American Tennis Association).

Soon, Ashe was entering, and winning, ATA tournaments. He dominated the ATA for eight years, from 1955 to 1963.

During those years, Ashe was as successful in the classroom as on the courts. He was an outstanding student at Booker T. Washington Jr. High and Maggie L. Walker High School.

When Ashe was a senior, he made an important choice. He moved to St. Louis so he could train with coach Richard Hudlin. He

At the age of 19, Arthur Ashe becomes the first African-American ever to play at the Wimbledon, England, tennis championship. He's shown making a return during his second round match on June 26, 1963.

finished school at Sumner High School in St. Louis. He had the highest grade-point average in his class.

COLLEGE: With great grades and great tennis skills Ashe won a scholarship to UCLA (University of California at Los Angeles).

There, he excelled in the classroom, earing a degree in business. On the tennis court, he led UCLA to a college championship.

Ashe was coached by Pancho Gonzalez, one of the greatest tennis players of all time. Under Gonzalez, Ashe got better and better. He became the first black player to play on the Davis Cup team.

The Davis Cup is an international competition. Tennis teams from countries all over the world play each other over many months. It is one of the most prestigious tournaments in the world. Ashe's Davis Cup play set a record. From 1963 to 1978, he won 27 singles matches and lost only five.

Ashe graduated from UCLA in 1966. It was cause for great celebration in the Ashe family. "I'll never forget how proud my grandmother was when I graduated from UCLA," he recalled. "Never mind the Davis Cup, Wimbledon. To this day she still doesn't know what those names mean. What mattered to her was that of her more than 30 children and grandchildren, I was the first to be graduated from college, and a famous college at that."

After college, Ashe served for two years in the Army Reserve. While in the Army, he coached the U.S. Military Academy tennis team.

SETTING RECORDS, BREAKING BARRIERS: Ashe took the tennis world by storm. In 1967, he won the U.S. Clay Court singles. (There are two kinds of matches in tennis, singles and doubles. In singles, two players play against one another. In doubles, teams of two players each play against one another.)

In 1968, he reached three important milestones. He became the first African-American to win the U.S. National men's singles. Next,

Ashe in the men's singles final at
Wimbledon, England, July 5, 1975.

he became the first black to win the U.S. Open. And that same year, he became the first African-American to be ranked #1 in U.S. tennis.

In 1969, the activist in Arthur Ashe began to take shape, too. He applied to play in the South African Open. At that time, South Africa was ruled by a racist white regime. They used the racist system of apartheid to deny South African blacks basic rights. Ashe was denied a visa to play in South Africa, because he was black. He took his case to the world. He called for South Africa to be thrown out of the international tennis organization. He was supported by people all over the world.

Throughout the 1970s, Ashe continued his winning ways. He won the Australian Open in 1970 and the WCT Championship in 1975.

In doubles play, Ashe was a champion, too. He won the U.S. Indoors doubles with Stan Smith in 1970. In 1971, he won the doubles championship at the French Open, with Marty Rieesen. In 1977, he won the Australian Open doubles with Tony Roche.

WIMBLEDON: One of the most prestigious tournaments in the world, in any sport, is Wimbledon. It's played at a famous tennis club in England. Ashe was the first African-American to play at Wimbledon, in 1963. In 1975, he proved his greatness once again, winning the singles crown against Jimmy Connors. He won 108 matches that year. Those stats led him to be named the Number One player in the world. He was the first black man to achieve that ranking.

HEALTH PROBLEMS: In 1979, Ashe suffered a heart attack. He had to have heart surgery. In 1980, he decided to retire from tennis. But he always kept his hand in the game. He continued as a coach for the Davis Cup team and as a writer and commentator on the game. And he continued to work to encourage African-American children to achieve in athletics and academics.

ACTIVISM: Ashe always encouraged minority children to play sports. He also wanted them to do well in school. He said communities should "build more libraries than gymnasiums." He gave tennis clinics all over the country. He spoke to government and community groups about the importance of education. He became involved with fighting racism all over the world.

Ashe was also a fine writer. He wrote newspaper columns and magazine articles. He also wrote three autobiographies and a history of black athletes, called *A Hard Road to Glory*.

AIDS: Ashe's health problems continued. He had to have heart surgery again in 1983. In 1988, he had to have an operation for a brain infection. That operation revealed that he had HIV, the virus that causes AIDS. Those letters stand for Human Immunodeficiency Virus and Acquired Immunodeficiency Syndrome. HIV-AIDS is a disease of the immune system. It is transferred by blood and other bodily fluids. Ashe was sure he had gotten the disease when he needed blood transfusions after heart surgery.

At that time, scientists were still trying to understand this deadly disease. Then, as now, there was no vaccine, and no cure, for AIDS. There were many people who shunned AIDS sufferers.

Because of this, Ashe kept his HIV status private, to protect his family. However, *USA Today* got hold of the story and published it, against his wishes. Ashe held a press conference and told the public he had AIDS.

Ashe immediately took action against the disease. He started the Arthur Ashe Foundation for the Defeat of AIDS. He spoke around the country and before the United Nations.

Ashe took a variety of medicines to slow the progress of his disease, but died on February 6, 1993, of AIDS-related pneumonia. He was 49 years old. His death was mourned around the world. He is remembered as a great man: an athlete, an activist, and a humanitarian dedicated to the betterment of humankind.

ARTHUR ASHE'S HOME AND FAMILY: Ashe married Jeanne Marie Moutoussamy in 1971. She is a photographer. They had one daughter, Camera Elizabeth. Ashe left her a series of letters to remember him by.

Arthur Ashe displays his trophy after defeating fellow American Jimmy Connors for the men's singles championship at the All England Lawn Tennis Championship in Wimbledon, England, July 5, 1975.

In 2006, Jeanne Moutoussamy-Ashe opened the Arthur Ashe Tennis and Education Center in East Falls, Pennsylvania. It is devoted to one of Ashe's lifetime goals: to help African-American children achieve in sports, school, and life.

In 2007, Jeanne created a web site devoted to her husband and his life. It's listed below. At the site, young readers can learn all about this great man, his legacy, and his values.

HIS LEGACY: After his death, writer Donna Doherty wrote about Ashe's legacy. "Arthur Ashe cast a spotlight across the paths of all he touched. He used tennis as his platform to spring into the business of trying to right the wrongs of this world. He would want us to do the same. To see beyond the tennis courts and learn to help others. To spend the time we have on earth making a difference, however small. It's the Arthur Ashe way."

WORLD WIDE WEB SITES:

http://www.arthurashe.org
http://www.cmgworldwide.com/sports/ashe/

CRISPUS ATTUCKS
PATRIOT

Crispus Attucks
1723(?) - 1770
African-American Patriot
First Person Killed at the Boston Massacre

CRISPUS ATTUCKS WAS BORN around 1723. He was born a slave in Massachusetts, and there is no record of his exact birthday. No one is exactly sure about his background and heritage. Some sources say that his father was Prince Younger, an African slave. Some say his mother was Nancy Attucks, a member of the Natick Indian tribe.

CRISPUS ATTUCKS GREW UP as a slave on a farm in Framingham, Massachusetts, historians believe. Sometime around the age of 27 he escaped slavery and became a sailor. He probably spent 20 years as a merchant seaman on whaling ships.

THE FIRST HERO OF THE AMERICAN REVOLUTION: In the 1770s, most of the area that is now the eastern United States was a colony of England. That means that the people were ruled by England. They paid taxes to the British government and were ruled by a king, George III.

Some of the colonists accepted English rule; others resented it. The British government had imposed stiff taxes on everyday items—like newspapers and even playing cards. The angry colonists rebelled.

In March 1770, Attucks was living in Boston. The colony was in an uproar over the British government's actions. British troops were stationed in the city to keep order. In this atmosphere of political and social turmoil, Attucks became one of the first heroes of what would become the Revolutionary War.

THE BOSTON MASSACRE: On the evening of March 5, 1770, a rumor began to fly around Boston. A British soldier had supposedly struck a young barber's apprentice. Armed only with snowballs and sticks, a group of citizens confronted the British soldiers. With Attucks at the head of the crowd, they marched to the Boston Customs House.

The soldiers fired into the crowd. When the smoke cleared, Crispus Attucks and three others lay dead. Eventually five men—Attucks, Samuel Gray, James Caldwell, Samuel Maverick, and Patrick Carr—died of their wounds.

The engraving by Paul Revere, depicting the Boston Massacre,
where Crispus Attucks died.

The people of Boston were furious. They claimed that Attucks and the other men were martyrs in the cause of independence. Attucks and Caldwell were given funerals that were attended by thousands of Boston's citizens. Despite racist laws that prevented blacks from being buried in white cemeteries, Attucks was buried in the Old Granary Burial Ground, with his fellow patriots.

Patriots like Samuel Adams called their murder "The Boston Massacre." It became a rallying cry in the years leading up to the

Revolutionary War (1775-1781).

Attucks became known to history as the "first to defy, the first to die" in the cause of liberty. John Adams, who became the second President of the United States, reluctantly defended the British soldiers at their murder trial.

HIS LEGACY: Attucks is remembered as one of the first heroes of the American Revolution. There is a monument in Boston Common that commemorates Attucks and his companions. The inscription says: "On that night, the foundation of American independence was laid." Paul Revere

Hours to the Gates of this City many Thoufands of our brave Brethren in the Country, deeply affected with our Diftreffes, and to whom we are greatly obliged on this Occafion—No one knows where this would have ended, and what important Confequences even to the whole British Empire might have followed, which our Moderation & Loyalty upon fo trying anOccafion, and ourFaith in the Commander'sAffurances have happily prevented.

Laft Thurfday, agreeable to a general Requeft of the Inhabitants, and by the Confent of Parents and Friends, were carried to their *Grave* in Succeffion, the Bodies of *Samuel Gray, Samuel Maverick, James Caldwell,* and *Crifpus Attucks,* the unhappy Victims who fell in the bloody Maffacre of theMonday Evening preceeding !

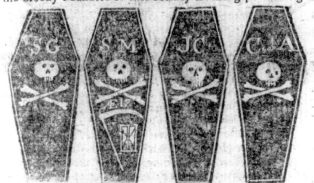

On this Occafion moft of the Shops in Town were fhut, all the Bells were ordered to toll a folemn Peal, as were alfo thofe in the neighboring Towns of Charleftown Roxbury, &c. The Proceffion began to move between the Hours of 4 and 5 in the Afternoon ; two of the unfortunate Sufferers, viz., Meff. *JamesCaldwell* and *Crifpus Attucks,* who were Strangers, borne from Faneuil-Hall,

1770 newspaper column about the Boston Massacre. The coffins in the illustration bear the initials of the four men killed: Samuel Gray, Samuel Maverick, James Caldwell, and Crispus Attucks.

made a famous engraving of the incident. That engraving rallied colonists to the revolutionary cause.

Attucks is also remembered as the first black to become a patriotic hero for African-Americans. That he became a martyr for liberty, when, as a black man, he was denied it, makes his sacrifice all the more meaningful.

Booker T. Washington wrote this about him in 1898: "When in 1776, the Negro was asked to decide between British oppression and American independence, we find him choosing the better part. Crispus Attucks, a Negro, was the first to shed his blood on State Street, Boston, that the white American might enjoy liberty forever, though his race remained in slavery."

Nearly 100 years later, Attucks's biographer James Neyland summed up his importance for our era: "He is one of the most important figures in African-American history, not for what he did for his own race, but for what he did for all oppressed people everywhere. He is a reminder that the African-American heritage is not only African but American and it is a heritage that begins with the beginning of America."

WORLD WIDE WEB SITES:

http://www.africawithin.com/bios/crispus_attucks.htm
http://www.memory.loc.gov/ammem/today/mar05.html
http://www.pbs.org/wgbh/aia/part2/2p24.html

Benjamin Banneker
1731 - 1806
African-American Astronomer,
Mathematician, and Inventor
Considered the First Black American Scientist

BENJAMIN BANNEKER WAS BORN on November 9, 1731, in Ellicott's Lower Mills, Maryland. His parents were Robert and Mary Banneker. Robert was born in West Africa. He had been enslaved and brought to Maryland. After years as a slave, he bought his freedom. Mary's father was a former slave from Africa. Her mother was an indentured servant from England. Both of them had won their freedom. Benjamin was born a free black, in an era when that was extremely rare.

MARYLAND IN THE 18TH CENTURY: Banneker was born before there was a United States. At the time of his birth, Maryland was one of several colonies ruled by Great Britain. He was also born when most black people in the colonies were slaves. Benjamin was one of only 200 free black people in a county where there were 4,000 slaves.

Robert and Mary Banneker were farmers. They worked land inherited from Mary's family. Benjamin was the oldest of three children. He had two younger sisters, Minta and Molly.

BENJAMIN BANNEKER GREW UP on the family farm. He was bright and curious, and loved learning everything about farming and tools. He was taught to read and write by his grandmother. He loved numbers, and enjoyed making up math games.

BENJAMIN BANNEKER WENT TO SCHOOL at a local Quaker school. The Quakers were a Christian group who believed in racial equality. The teacher encouraged Benjamin, and he was an excellent student. No one is sure how many years he went to school. He probably left in his teens.

CLOCK MAKER: Around 1753, Banneker saw a watch for the first time. He was fascinated. He took the watch apart, and studied how it worked. Then, he built his own clock, entirely out of wood. It is considered the first wooden clock built in the New World. It kept time for 40 years.

ALMANAC: Banneker inherited the family farm when his father died in 1757. He learned all he could about farming techniques. That included studying rain and weather patterns. He also examined the movement of the stars. A neighbor, George Ellicott, lent Banneker books on astronomy and math. From this research, he developed an "Almanac."

An almanac is a collection of data that includes information about weather, seasons, tides, sunrises, sunsets, and other natural happenings. In Banneker's time, they were used by farmers, sailors, and others for planning harvesting, shipping, and fishing. Banneker's almanac also included bits of history, literature, poems, and proverbs.

Banneker published his almanac from 1792 to 1797. They were a great success. He sent a copy to Thomas Jefferson, who was then Secretary of State for President George Washington. Banneker included a letter to Jefferson challenging his racist views. Jefferson believed that black people were inferior to white people. Jefferson responded to Banneker, thanking him for the almanac. He also acknowledged that Banneker had changed his thinking.

Title page from Benjamin Banneker's first Almanac, 1792.

SURVEYOR: In 1791, the new capital of the new United States was being built in Washington, DC. The architect hired to plan the city was Pierre-Charles L'Enfant. Banneker was hired to be part of the six-man team to survey the new city. They were in charge of planning out the streets, buildings, and general outline of the city.

L'Enfant quit suddenly, taking the plans with him. The team was in trouble. But Banneker saved the day. He reconstructed L'Enfant's plan, completely from memory.

BENJAMIN BANNEKER'S HOME AND FAMILY: Banneker never married. He lived on his farm with his sisters until his death. Over the years his health failed, and he had to sell off most of the land. Tragically, when he died on October 9, 1806, his house burned down. All his books, and his clock, perished in the fire.

HIS LEGACY: Banneker is considered the first black scientist in the U.S. His clock is considered the first working wooden clock built in the New World.

WORLD WIDE WEB SITES:

http://www.benjaminbanneker.org/about_bbhas/benjamin_banneker.htm
http://www.pbs.org/wgbh/aia/part2/2p84.html
http://www.web.mit.edu/invent/iow/Banneker.html

Mary McLeod Bethune
1875 - 1955
African-American Educator and Civil Rights Activist

MARY BETHUNE WAS BORN on July 10, 1875, in Mayesville, South Carolina. Bethune became her last name when she married. Her name when she was born was Mary Jane McLeod. (Her last name is pronounced "muh-CLOUD.") Her parents were Samuel McLeod and Patsy McIntosh. They had been slaves on a cotton plantation until 1865. That year, when the **CIVIL WAR** ended, and they became free.

After the war, the McLeods continued to work for their former owners, as tenant farmers. They saved their earnings and bought five acres of farmland near Mayesville. They built a log cabin that they named "The Homestead."

Mary Jane was her parents' 15th child, and the first to be born free. Most of her older brothers and sisters had been sold into slavery as infants. After the war, those brothers and sisters came home. The family was finally reunited.

MARY BETHUNE GREW UP in a family that knew hard times even after they were freed. All the children worked hard in the fields. They grew food to eat and cotton to sell. Mary was a hard worker. It was said that by the time she was nine years old she could pick 250 pounds of cotton in a day.

The McLeods were a religious family. The children were taught that God rewards those who have a strong faith and work hard to help others. The Homestead became a welcome gathering place for friends and neighbors. As a child, Mary saw her parents share what little they had with others.

A SEGREGATED WORLD: One day Mary went with her mother to deliver laundry to her former owner. She was invited to play with the women's white grandchildren. Among the bright, shiny new toys was something that caught Mary's eye. It was a book. When she reached out to pick it up one of the white children told her, "Put that down. *You* can't read."

The experience with the book changed Mary forever. She promised herself that she would learn to read one day. In later years, Bethune said that the white girl's words made her see the importance of education. She began to wonder if the reason white people had better houses and a better way of life was because they knew how to read and write.

EARLY SCHOOLING: Mary finally got her chance to go to school. A Presbyterian mission group sent Emma Jane Wilson to Mayesville to open a school for former slaves. Mary eagerly walked five miles to the one-room schoolhouse. Here she realized her dream and learned to read.

Now when she went with her father to sell the cotton they'd picked, she could tell when the buyer was cheating them. Since she could read the weight on the scale, when the buyer told her father that he had 280 pounds, she corrected him by saying, "Isn't it 480 pounds?"

In 1886, when she was 11 years old, Mary had gone as far as she could at the Mayesville missionary school. Because there were no other schools nearby, she returned to the cotton fields to work with her parents. But because she could now read, write, add, and subtract, she could help other farmers get fair prices for their crops.

When Mary was 12, her former teacher visited the McLeods. She told them that a women named Mary Chrissman wanted to offer a scholarship to one of the Mayesville mission school students to continue their education. Mary McLeod received the scholarship.

Generous neighbors helped supply Mary with the school supplies and clothing she would need to attend the Scotia Seminary in Concord, North Carolina. The day she left on the train, the whole community went to the station to send her off.

The Scotia Seminary seemed elegant to Mary. Brick buildings with glass windows, white tablecloths and water glasses—these were things unknown to her. She was also surprised to find black and white teachers sitting side by side at the tables.

Mary made friends easily and quickly became a leader among the students. She was a good student and had a beautiful singing voice. In 1890 she was promoted to the Normal and Scientific Course where she studied to become a teacher. She also had a goal to become a missionary and go to Africa.

THE MOODY BIBLE INSTITUTE: Before graduating from Scotia, Mary applied to the Moody Bible Institute in Chicago. She felt that proper Bible study would help her achieve her goal of going to Africa. Once again, Miss Chrissman paid the tuition.

Mary arrived in Chicago to find herself the only African-American among 1,000 students. But it was here, Mary later said, that she learned "a love for the whole human race." She studied hard and found her faith deepening.

At the end of her study at Moody, Mary applied to the Presbyterian Mission for an assignment in Africa. But there were no positions available for an African-American missionary.

Mary returned home to Mayesville and became an assistant teacher with Emma Wilson, her former teacher. One year later she took a teaching position at the Haines Normal and Industrial Institute in Augusta, Georgia.

A YOUNG TEACHER: Lucy Craft Laney, a black educator and the first woman to graduate from Atlanta University, founded the

Haines Institute. Bethune taught eighth grade there. In her spare time, she helped families in the poor community surrounding the school.

Bethune also became a Sunday school teacher with an unusual program. On Sunday mornings she and her students went to the homes of the poor. They bathed children and gave out clothing, soap, toothbrushes, combs, and towels.

Inspired by Lucy Laney, Mary discovered her new mission. She became determined to work toward providing education for young black girls—in her own country.

MARRIAGE AND MOTHERHOOD: In 1897, at the age of 22, Mary took another teaching position at the Kindell Institute in Sumter, South Carolina. While singing in the choir, she met a fellow teacher named Albertus Bethune. Within a year they were married and soon moved to Savannah, Georgia. In 1899 their son, Albertus McLeod Bethune, was born. Mary took time off from teaching to take care of her baby.

MOVING TO FLORIDA: Six months after Albertus's birth, a pastor from Palatka, Florida, asked Mary to teach at his school. Her husband encouraged her to take the offer. With infant son in tow, Bethune moved to Florida. Once again she organized a Sunday school program and sang in the choir.

Bethune began reading about **Booker T. Washington**. He was a former slave who had founded the Tuskegee Normal and Industrial Institute in Alabama. Washington believed that blacks could better themselves and their lives by learning practical skills like farming and carpentry. At his Institute and through workshops and fairs,

Washington educated thousands of black farmers. His writings inspired Bethune. They fueled her passion to start her own school for black girls.

DAYTONA BEACH: Construction on the Florida East Coast Railway provided work for black laborers who came from all over the South. The children of these workers needed a school. In 1904, Bethune and her young son took a train from Palatka to Daytona Beach. She had only $1.50 in cash. But she had a burning desire to create a school.

Bethune noticed that all the towns she saw had something in common. They all had a black section and a white section. And the black section was always the poorer of the two. When she reached Daytona Beach and walked through the black section she knew this would be the perfect place to start her school.

THE DAYTONA NORMAL AND INDUSTRIAL INSTITUTE FOR NEGRO GIRLS: On October 4, 1904, Mary McLeod Bethune rang a bell to signal the opening of her school. She'd rented a two-story cottage by the railroad tracks with her $1.50. Five little girls, ages eight to 12, were the first students. Tuition was 50 cents a month.

But even as the school accepted more and more students, the tuition was not enough to pay all the bills. Bethune asked for help from community members. She raised money and found supplies wherever she could. She looked through the dump and trash piles. She wrote letters to wealthy vacationers in Daytona Beach. One man, James Gamble, was impressed with Bethune. He became a strong supporter, donating money and legal services. He was the son of one of the founders of Proctor & Gamble.

Within two years the school had 250 students. Bethune needed more space. She found a piece of land in the black section of town for sale for $200.00. The owner agreed to sell it to her with only $5.00 down. Volunteers cleaned up the land while Bethune found donations of bricks and lumber.

In October of 1907 the school moved to its new site. The motto of the school was displayed over the doorways: "Enter to Learn. Depart to Serve."

Bethune began speaking at hotels, asking rich vacationers to help her school. One gentleman gave her a $20 bill, a lot of money in those days. The next day he came to Mary's school and asked for a tour. He came back the next morning with a brand new sewing machine and workmen to finish the main building. The man was Thomas H. White of Dayton, Ohio, owner of the White Sewing Machine Company.

Throughout the years White was a regular visitor to the school and helped with gifts of money. He and James Gamble even got together and bought a two-story house for Bethune. She called it "The Retreat" and lived there until she died.

But Bethune's husband was unhappy. He felt she was spending too much time trying to help others instead of concentrating on her family. In 1908 Albertus Bethune left Mary and their son and moved to South Carolina. He died in 1919 without ever seeing them again.

SEPARATE BUT NOT EQUAL: Even as a young girl Bethune realized that black people did not have the same opportunities that white people did. Her school was the first of her efforts to help

Mary Bethune in front of White Hall at Bethune-Cookman College, Daytona Beach, Fla.

improve the quality of life for the children of former slaves.

She worked tirelessly to help those in need. One project saw the students from The Daytona Institute teaching black laborers in the turpentine camps how to read and write.

When a student at the Daytona School became ill with appendicitis, she was not allowed to go into the nearest hospital because she was black. Bethune pleaded with the white doctor to treat the girl and he finally agreed. After the operation Bethune went to visit the young girl and found she was not being cared for.

Bethune took action. She bought a small house and converted it into a hospital. She caught the attention of Andrew Carnegie, one of the wealthiest men in America. He gave Bethune the money she needed to complete the hospital. She named it after her mother, Patsy McLeod. It had only two beds when it opened. Before long it grew into a 26-bed hospital.

In 1908, Booker T. Washington visited Bethune's school. They talked about their goals as teachers. Both dreamed of a world where blacks would have the same rights as whites and become leaders in America. They both knew that education was the key

Mary Bethune turns the presidency of Bethune-
Cookman College over to James Colston, 1943.

and hoped that the work they were doing would help this dream come true.

In 1923, the Daytona Normal Institute merged with the Cookman Institute in Jacksonville, Florida, a school for boys. The merger helped save both schools. When Bethune-Cookman College opened it doors, Bethune knew she had accomplished what she had set out to do. She served as college president until 1943.

A WOMAN OF FIRSTS: Bethune spent her entire life working to help African- Americans achieve the same rights as white people.

She strongly believed in the words "All people are created equal." She traveled the country speaking out for equality.

A woman of incredible energy and accomplishment, Bethune helped to change society in many ways. During World War I, she helped integrate the Red Cross. In the 1930s, President Franklin D. Roosevelt named her Director of the Office of Negro Affairs. She became the first African-American and the first woman ever run a national agency.

Bethune founded the National Council of Negro Women in 1935. Its purpose is to promote community support for African-American women.

Mary Bethune with singer Marian Anderson
and a group of soldiers, at the launch of
the SS Booker T. Washington, the first Liberty Ship
to be named for an African-American, 1943.

Bethune also helped integrate the armed forces. As a result of her efforts, 10 percent of the officers in the Women's Army Auxiliary Corps (WAAC) were African-American women. She established a pilot training program at Tuskegee University that graduated black pilots who fought in World War II.

LAST DAYS: In 1952 Bethune was finally able to travel to Africa. She visited the nation of Liberia and attended the inauguration of its president. She spoke at the American Embassy and was awarded the country's Star of Africa medal.

But her health was failing. She spent her last days at her home, the Retreat. She died on May 18, 1955, at the age of 79. She was buried on the campus of Bethune-Cookman College.

HER LEGACY: Bethune is remembered as a tireless advocate for equality for African-Americans. She was determined to provide equal education to blacks, and spoke out about the rights of minorities and women. In 1974, A bronze statue of Mary McLeod Bethune was dedicated in Washington, D.C., the first monument to an African-American, and the first to a woman, in the nation's capitol.

WORLD WIDE WEB SITES:

http://www.lkwdpl.org/wihohio/beth-mar.htm
http://www.nahc.org/NAHC/
http://www.nps.org
http://www.usca.edu/aasc/bethune.htm

Jim Brown
1936 -
African-American Professional Football Player,
Actor, and Activist

JIM BROWN WAS BORN on February 17, 1936, in St. Simons Island, Georgia. His full name is James Nathaniel Brown. His parents were Swinton and Theresa Brown. Swinton, a professional boxer, left the family when Jim was an infant. Theresa had to move north to find work, so Jim was raised by his great-grandmother in his early years. His mother sent for him when he was eight.

JIM BROWN GREW UP first in Georgia, then in New York. His mother had found work as a domestic in Manhasset, New York. The two of them lived there through his high school years.

JIM BROWN WENT TO SCHOOL first in Georgia, where he went to a segregated school that was a two-room shack. After moving to New York to live with his mother, he attended the public schools in Manhasset. He recalled that he got into a fight on his first day at Manhasset Valley Elementary. "My mother had dressed me in new clothes," he remembered. During recess, another boy said he looked "pretty" and shoved him. "I reacted Georgia-style," Brown said. "I tackled him, pinned him with my knees, punched him. The closed circle of kids watching then started chanting, 'Dirty fighter.' I stopped fighting. I was mystified. How did these boys fight up here?"

Soon, Jim became a more welcome part of the school community. He did well in school, and was an outstanding athlete, too. At Manhasset High, he earned 13 letters in football, basketball, baseball, track, and lacrosse. He was also an honor student, and elected to be chief justice of his high school's student court.

All his success in the classroom and on the field didn't keep him out of trouble, though. He joined a gang, and got involved in fights.

SYRACUSE UNIVERSITY: Brown had many options for college, and chose Syracuse University. On a football scholarship, Brown became a star in football and basketball. But not before he faced racial discrimination on the field.

During his first year of college, Brown was benched in favor of white players with less talent. He finally got his chance to play after one of the white players got injured. He used the opportunity to show what he could do. In his sophomore year, he was second in team rushing. In basketball, he had the second highest scoring average. He added a letter in track that year, too. As a junior, he lettered in football, basketball, and lacrosse.

In his senior year, Brown was a two-time All-American, in football and lacrosse. He led his team to the Cotton Bowl that year, where Syracuse lost to Texas Christian. By then Brown had established himself as one of the great college football players of his era. He graduated from Syracuse in 1957 and began his pro career.

THE CLEVELAND BROWNS: Brown was the first-round draft pick of the Cleveland Browns in 1957. Right away, he became a star running back. In his first year with the Browns, his 942 yards rushing led all running backs in the league. He received the NFL's Rookie of the Year award, and Most Valuable Player, too.

In 1958, Brown led the league in rushing with 1,527 yards. He also led all other running backs in touchdowns, with 18. In 1959, Brown rushed for 1,329 yards, and in 1960 for 1,257 yards. Both were league-leading stats. The next year, Brown did it again, leading the league with a whopping 1,408 yards rushing. In fact, he won the rushing record in all his nine seasons as a pro except for one, 1962.

That season, Brown voiced his disappointment with coach Paul Brown. He threatened to quit if Brown didn't leave. The coach was fired. The next season, 1963, saw Jim Brown make it into the record books again, as the first running back to run for 1,863 yards. His 1964 season was even more spectacular: he led the Browns to the NFL championship, and led the league with 1,446 yards.

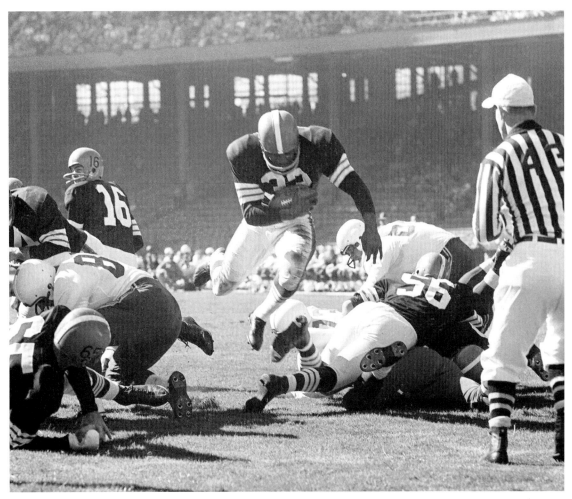

*Brown runs for a touchdown during a game against the Chicago Cardinals,
October 12, 1958, in Cleveland, Ohio.*

The 1965 season would be Brown's last in the NFL. He went out
on top, as the rushing leader (with 1,544 yards) and touchdown
leader (21).

Brown left the game with 15,459 total yards, a record that stood
for years. He was a first- team All-NFL pick every year except one.
He played in the Pro Bowl every year of his career, and was MVP
four times: 1957, 1958, 1963, and 1965. And he never missed a game
in all nine years. It's a career that's made him a legend in football.

STARTING TO MAKE MOVIES: In 1966, Brown was working on one of his best-known films, *The Dirty Dozen*, when he announced his retirement from football. His announcement stunned the world, but Brown said he was ready for other challenges. "I quit with regret but not sorrow," he said. "I've been able to do all the things I wanted to do. Now I want to devote my time to other things. And I wanted more mental stimulation than I would have had playing football."

Over the years, he made many movies, including *Dark of the Sun* and *Ice Station Zebra*. While building his movie career, he also became involved in community development.

GETTING INVOLVED IN THE COMMUNITY: While he was still playing football, Brown started the Black Economic Union. Its purpose was to help African-Americans start their own businesses. Later, he formed Amer-I-can. That organization seeks to help gang members and prisoners to improve their lives. He hopes that other African-American athletes will join him in this effort.

HALL OF FAME HONORS: The fans didn't forget Jim Brown, even though he'd gone on to other things. In 1971, he was inducted into the Pro Football Hall of Fame. He was also inducted into the Hall of Fame for College Football and Lacrosse. No other athlete has been so honored. In 2005, Syracuse University retired his number, 44.

PERSONAL PROBLEMS: Brown has been plagued by problems in his personal life for many years. He has been accused of assault charges, and several of his partners have accused him of domestic violence. Brown served a four-month jail term for assault in 2005.

Jim Brown is honored during halftime of the Rutgers-Syracuse game, October 5, 1996, at the Carrier Dome in Syracuse, New York.

JIM BROWN'S HOME AND FAMILY: Brown has been married twice. His first wife was named Sue. They had three children together, Kim, Kevin, and Jim Jr. His second wife is named Monique.

HIS LEGACY: Brown is considered one of the finest running backs to ever play football. Sports commentator Bob Costas summed up his career. "5.2 yards per carry, never missed a game, won the rushing title every year but one. There are a lot of contenders, but if you had to select one, you have to pick Jim as the greatest running back in history."

WORLD WIDE WEB SITES:

http://espn.go/com/classic/biography/s/Brown_Jim.html
http://www.profootballhof.com/hof/member.jsp?player_id=33
http://www.sportsplacement.com/brownbio.htm

Ralph Bunche
1903 - 1971
African-American Statesman,
Scholar, and Civil Rights Leader
First Person of Color to Win the Nobel Prize for Peace

RALPH BUNCHE WAS BORN on August 7, 1903, in Detroit, Michigan. His full name was Ralph Johnson Bunche. His parents were Fred and Olive Bunche. Fred was a barber and Olive was a home-maker and amateur musician. Ralph had two sisters.

RALPH BUNCHE GREW UP in several places. His family moved often, for his father's work and his mother's health. During his early years, he lived in Michigan, Ohio, and Tennessee.

Ralph Bunche as a baby

RALPH BUNCHE WENT TO SCHOOL in all those places, as the family moved around. In 1914, they moved to Albuquerque, New Mexico. Ralph was an excellent student, although one of his early teachers said he liked to talk in class.

Sadly, by the time he was 14, both Ralph's parents were dead. He moved to Los Angeles, where he lived with his grandmother. Ralph said she was a great influence on him. She always encouraged him to do his best, and to succeed. When school officials wanted to put Ralph in a "general" high school program because he was black, she put her foot down. She insisted he be given tough academic courses, because he was going to college.

Ralph proved his grandmother right. He was an outstanding student, and also a fine athlete and debater. In 1922, Bunche graduated from Jefferson High School first in his class. He faced racial discrimination again that year. The city's honor society wouldn't let him be a member, because he was black. But he didn't let that stop his plans.

Bunche won a scholarship to the University of California at Los Angeles (UCLA). There, he studied political science. That's the study of government and politics. He was an excellent student, and an athlete, too. He played baseball, basketball, and football at

UCLA. He also worked to help pay for his education. Bunche graduated from college, again at the top of his class, in 1927.

Bunche went on to graduate school at Harvard University. He studied political science, and received his master's degree in 1928. That same year, Bunche began teaching at Howard University. He started the school's political science department. He combined teaching with working on a Ph.D. in Government and International Relations at Harvard. As part of his research, he traveled to Africa. That experience helped to determine his life's work. Bunche completed his Ph.D. in 1934. He was the first African-American to earn a doctoral degree in his field from Harvard.

Ralph Bunche was an outstanding athlete at UCLA, playing basketball, football, and baseball.

In a career that spanned more than 40 years, Bunche had three main interests. He was devoted to Civil Rights in his own country, to helping nations of Africa achieve self-government, and to peace in the Middle East.

GETTING INVOLVED IN CIVIL RIGHTS: Bunche was actively involved in the **CIVIL RIGHTS MOVEMENT.** He had suffered from discrimination first hand, so he knew the problems facing blacks. He'd faced it in school, when he was denied membership in his high school's honor society. Later, as a high-ranking government officer, he couldn't buy a house in restricted areas of Washington, D.C.

Bunche believed that African-Americans needed to join together and fight for equal rights. He felt that racism was wrong everywhere, in the U.S. and the world. In 1936, he helped to form the National Negro Congress. That was an early African-American group that fought for equal rights.

Bunche served on the board of the **NAACP (NATIONAL ASSOCIATION FOR THE ADVANCEMENT OF COLORED PEOPLE)** for 22 years. In 1949, the organization gave him the Springarn Medal, its most important award. He was a powerful speaker and writer on Civil Rights, too. He wrote a book in 1936 about segregation in the U.S. He joined **Martin Luther King Jr.** for the march on Washington in 1963 and the march from Selma to Montgomery in 1965. An honored leader, Bunche was given the Medal of Freedom by President John F. Kennedy in 1963.

SCHOLAR AND TEACHER: As a scholar, Bunche taught at Howard University from 1928 to 1950. He also taught at Harvard and served on the Board of Education in New York City.

PUBLIC SERVANT: Bunche is best known as one of the finest public servants of the 20th century. Beginning in 1941, and continuing until his death in 1971, he served the U.S. government and the United Nations as a tireless advocate for peace and human rights.

In 1941, President Franklin Roosevelt named Bunche the African specialist for the Office of Strategic Services. In that job, he was able to promote his deeply-held belief that nations need to determine their own futures. At that time, many of the countries of Africa were colonies of Western European nations. As such, they were not in control of their own governments. Bunche's goal was to lead the nations of Africa to self-determination.

Ralph Bunche meets with Kwame Nkrumah,
Prime Minister of Ghana, 1958.

In 1944, Bunche joined the U.S. State Department. That is the division of government that determines and directs U.S. foreign policy all over the world. **Condoleezza Rice** and **Colin Powell** have served as Secretary of State, the title of the head of the State Department.

Bunche became the first African-American to head a division of the State Department. He was named chief of the Division of Dependent Affairs in 1945.

JOINING THE UNITED NATIONS: In 1945, Bunche helped to write the "Charter," or governing document, that established the United Nations (UN). The next year, he became Director of the UN Trusteeship Division. In that job, he helped former colonies achieve self-government. The process was called "decolonization," and Bunche was its champion.

Bunche stated his goals: "To provide for the economic, social, and political development of the peoples in trust territories to insure their rights and their freedoms and set as an ultimate goal their self-government or independence."

WORKING FOR PEACE IN THE MIDDLE EAST: Bunche next worked on one of the most difficult issues in modern world politics. In 1947, he became involved in the recognition of the new nation of Israel. The country of Israel is on territory that has been fought over for centuries. After Israel was created, angry bordering nations began a war. That conflict, known as the Arab-Israeli War, raged from 1948 to 1949.

Bunche was called upon to find peace among the warring nations. He worked on the final agreement, and helped end the conflict in 1949. For his efforts, he won the Nobel Prize.

THE NOBEL PEACE PRIZE: In 1950, Bunche was awarded the Nobel Peace Prize. That is one of the most important awards in the world. It is given every year to the individual, or individuals, who

*Martin Luther King, Jr., Coretta Scott King, and Ralph Bunche
at the United Nations, 1963.*

work for peace. He was the first person of color to receive the award.

LATER CAREER: In 1955, Bunche became the undersecretary of the UN. In that role, he led the UN's peacekeeping forces around the world. The Secretary General of the UN, Dag Hammarskjold, named Bunche to head the International Atomic Energy Agency. In particular, Bunche worked to insure that the world would develop nuclear energy for peaceful uses.

RALPH BUNCHE'S HOME AND FAMILY: Bunche met his future wife, Ruth Harris, at Howard University. They married in 1930. They had three children, Joan, Jane, and Ralph, Jr.

In bad health, Bunche retired from the UN in 1971. He died shortly after his retirement, on December 9, 1971. He was 68 years old.

HIS LEGACY: Bunche is remembered as an outstanding statesman devoted to Civil Rights at home and peace throughout the world. He was brilliant and compassionate, and dedicated those gifts to the service of humanity. Throughout his career, he remained positive about his mission. "I am a professional optimist. If I were not a professional optimist through 21 years of UN service, I would be crazy. You have to be optimistic in this work or get out of it. That is, optimistic in the sense of assuming that there is no problem which cannot be solved."

WORLD WIDE WEB SITES:

http://nobelprize.org/
http://www.pbs.org/ralphbunche/
http://www.ralphbunchcentenary.org
http://www.thepeacemission.com/ralph-bunche.htm

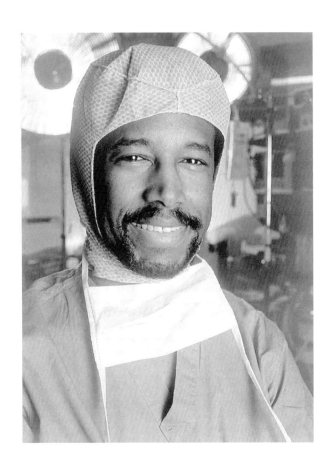

Ben Carson
1951 -
African-American Neurosurgeon and Author

BEN CARSON WAS BORN on September 18, 1951, in Detroit, Michigan. His full name is Benjamin Solomon Carson. His parents were Robert and Sonya Carson. He has one older brother, Curtis.

BEN CARSON GREW UP in Detroit in a poor family and a rough neighborhood. His parents divorced when Ben was eight. Ben and Curtis lived with their mom. Sonya Carson worked long hours cleaning houses to support her family. Money was tight. Carson remembers that "whenever Curtis or I asked for toys or candy, we heard the same answer: 'we just don't have the money'."

BEN CARSON WENT TO SCHOOL at Higgins Elementary in Detroit. He didn't like school, and he didn't do well, either. He thought he was the "dumbest kid in school." Kids teased him, and he faced racism, too. White kids threatened him at school, on the playground, and even walking home. It made him sad, and angry, too.

Then his mom stepped in and made some changes. Sonya Carson had only gone to school through the third grade, but she knew the importance of education. She thought Ben and Curtis weren't doing well in school because they watched too much TV. So she limited them to three hours a week.

Instead, the boys had to read two books a week. They also had to write a book report on each book. The boys complained, but the extra reading made a difference. Ben went from the bottom to the top of his class.

At Wilson Junior High, Carson won an award as the highest-achieving student. But he still faced racism. At the awards assembly, a teacher "bawled out the white kids because they had allowed me to be number one," Carson recalled.

Despite his success in school, Carson was often angry and unhappy. As a teenager, he sometimes let his hot temper get the best of him. He fought with his brother and with friends. Once, he tried to stab a friend in anger. Luckily for everyone, the knife broke against the friend's belt. The friend was unharmed, and Ben had a chance to change.

The incident really turned Carson around. He shut himself in the bathroom and read the Bible. "It said that mightier is the person who can control his temper than the one who can run the city," he recalled. "I realized I was my own worst enemy and that a weak person is controlled by anger."

Guided by his religious faith and his mother's love, Carson set out to be the best person he could be. He was an outstanding student at Southwestern High School. He played in the band and worked in the lab after school. He did so well that he won a scholarship to Yale University, one of the best colleges in the country.

DECIDING TO BECOME A DOCTOR: Carson studied hard at Yale. College was tough, but he was determined to do well. He majored in psychology and decided he wanted to be a doctor. After graduating in 1973, he went to medical school at the University of Michigan. When he started med school, Carson planned to become a psychiatrist. (A psychiatrist has a medical degree and specializes in human psychology.) As part of his medical training, he studied surgery. He loved it. Carson decided to become a neurosurgeon.

BECOMING A NEUROSURGEON: "Neurology" is the study of the brain, spinal cord, and nerves. A neurosurgeon specializes in operations in this incredibly important—and delicate—area of the body. Neurosurgeons deal with life-threatening conditions—like a tumor growing in the brain or an injury to the spinal cord.

After finishing medical school in 1977, Carson continued his training at Johns Hopkins in Baltimore, Maryland. That is one of the finest medical facilities in the world. During his training, he spent a year at a hospital in Australia. There, he performed several brain surgeries. He removed tumors from patient's brains that allowed them to lead normal lives.

Carson with a young patient.

CHIEF OF PEDIATRIC NEUROSURGERY: Returning to Johns Hopkins in 1984, Carson was named chief of "pediatric neurosurgery." That is a neurosurgeon who specializes in children's needs. His patients had many serious medical problems. Some had brain tumors, and some suffered from seizures and other serious conditions.

The brain controls almost all movement and behavior. Scientists are still discovering exactly how each part of the brain works, but they do know what happens when things go wrong. A tumor can press on areas of the brain that control speech and movement. Seizures can cause brain damage and death.

In one case, Carson performed surgery on a four-year-old girl who was having over 100 seizures a day. He removed a portion of her brain. The little girl recovered completely, and now lives a normal life.

A FAMOUS OPERATION: One of Carson's most serious cases involved a pair of twins, Patrick and Benjamin. They were "conjoined" twins, who were born with the back of their heads grown together. Conjoined twins are separate infants who share some body parts. (Twins born connected in this way are sometimes called Siamese twins.) Surgery to separate them is very difficult and risky.

Carson's job was to try to separate the twins, including the brain and surrounding blood vessels. The surgery had never been performed successfully. There was a large risk that both babies might die, or suffer brain damage.

The operation took place on September 5, 1987. Carson headed a team of 70 doctors and nurses. It took 22 hours to separate the boys, but Carson and his team did it.

The success of the operation made Carson famous. He became known around the world for his skill. And as people learned of his achievement in medicine, they also learned of his life story. Many were moved by his journey to success.

"I came to understand that the life I've had is unusual," remembers Carson. "Many people who have yet to achieve could probably identify with it. My biggest mission was to see if perhaps something could be done, using the example of my life, to encourage others to develop a "can do" as opposed to a "what-can-you-do-for-me" attitude."

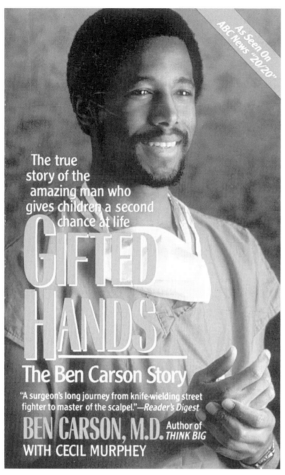

Carson has written many books about his remarkable life.

To share his story, Carson wrote several books about his remarkable life. In books like *Gifted Hands, THINK BIG,* and *The Big Picture*, he tells how he achieved his dreams. But most importantly, he encourages people, especially young people, to make their own dreams come true.

"Think big," says Carson, referring to his book. "Each letter in the two words represents something: **T**alent, **H**onesty, **In**sight, **N**ice, **K**nowledge; **B**ooks, **In**-depth learning, and **G**od. I guarantee that anyone who follows those tips will succeed."

Carson continues to perform 500 to 600 surgeries every year. He still loves his work. His favorite part is telling the worried parents of a patient: "Your child is awake and asking for you." "To me, that is a highlight," says Carson. "I love it."

BEN CARSON'S HOME AND FAMILY: Carson met his wife, Candy, while he was in college. She is a musician. They have three sons, Murray, Ben Jr., and Rhoeyce. The family lives near Baltimore with three generations of Carsons: Ben and Candy, their sons, and Ben's mom, Sonya.

Carson speaks to a group of young students.

Carson visits schools and youth groups often. He tells children about his own life. He wants them to know that they can achieve whatever they want, if they're willing to work hard. "The person who has the most to do with what happens to you is you," he says. He and his wife started a scholarship program, the Carson Scholars Fund. It provides money for college scholarships for kids.

Carson is a very religious man. He believes that faith has guided his life and his success. "God's hand is still at work in my life," he says. "Do your best, and let God do the rest."

HIS LEGACY: Through his ground-breaking work as a surgeon, and his compassion toward all people, Carson has become a role model for African-Americans. He is devoted to helping young people be all they can be.

WORLD WIDE WEB SITES:

http://www.achievement.org/autodoc/page/car1int1
http://www.drbencarson.com
http://www.topblacks.com/medicine/ben-carson.htm
http://www.carolina.com/carson/index.asp

George Washington Carver
1864(?) - 1943
**African-American Inventor, Farmer,
Educator and Food Scientist
Created more than 300 Products Using Peanuts**

GEORGE WASHINGTON CARVER WAS BORN in the Kansas Territory near Diamond Grove, Missouri. He was born a slave. George's mother, Mary, had been sold as a slave for $700 when she was 13. The German couple who owned her, Moses and Susan Carver, treated her as a farm hand rather than a slave. They gave Mary a small cabin on the farm.

Mary worked with Susan in the house and the garden. Because birth records were not kept on slaves, the exact date of George's birth is not known. However, it is likely he was born in 1864, near the end of the **CIVIL WAR**. There isn't a record of his father's name. It is believed that his father was a slave on a neighboring farm, who died in an accident shortly after George's birth.

At the beginning of the Civil War, in 1861, the South seceded from the Union. The country was divided, North and South, on the issue of slavery. The Northern states wanted to preserve the Union and abolish slavery. The Southern states wanted slavery to continue, and to extend into the territories. Because Missouri bordered states allied with both the North and South, soldiers from both sides fought bloody battles not far from Diamond Grove.

One night a band of soldiers rode onto Moses Carver's farm and kidnapped Mary and her baby, George. The soldiers took them to Arkansas. Moses Carver sent a man to find them but he returned with only George. No one ever knew what happened to Mary. George grew up never knowing his mother.

The Carvers had no children of their own. They raised George as their own son, even giving him their last name.

GEORGE WASHINGTON CARVER GREW UP where almost everything the family needed came from the farm. They grew fruits and vegetables, raised livestock, and spun fabric for clothing from flax and wool. Moses Carver was also a bee keeper with more than 50 hives.

George was a sickly child who suffered from breathing problems. He was also small for his age. He helped Susan plant and weed the gardens. He picked fruit, milked cows, and gathered eggs from the hens. He also helped in the house doing laundry, cleaning, and cooking.

George loved working in the garden and exploring the woods. He liked learning to do new things and was always asking questions. He went to Sunday school every week. He loved playing marbles and went swimming and fishing with the other children in Diamond Grove.

THE PLANT DOCTOR: George developed a keen interest in plants at an early age. He wondered why some flowers grew in the sun and some in the shade. He noticed that plants with the same roots produced flowers that were different colors. He collected leaves, seeds, and tree bark. He took care of the flowers around the Carver house so carefully that people began asking him how they could make their own gardens thrive. "Love them," was his answer.

Soon people were bringing their sick plants to Carver. His careful attention to the details of nature helped him learn how to nurse sick plants back to health. He became known as "The Plant Doctor" in Diamond Grove.

EARLY SCHOOLING: Before the Civil War there were laws against teaching slaves to read and write. After the war, African-Americans supposedly gained the right to an education. But George was not allowed to attend the local school because he was black. Missouri's racist laws allowed schools to bar blacks from attending. That is what happened to George.

George taught himself to read from a copy of "Webster's Elementary Spelling Book." Moses Carver hired the village school teacher to tutor him. But George wanted more. So when he was about 12 years old, he left the farm and walked eight miles to Neosho, Missouri, where there was a one-room schoolhouse that he could attend.

In Neosho, George stayed with an African-American couple, Andrew and Mariah Watkins, who had no children of their own. Andrew did odd jobs around town and Mariah worked as a midwife and laundry woman. When she had to leave home to help someone have a baby, George took over the cooking and the laundry. They lived next door to the school. During recess George didn't play with the other children. Instead, he walked home to help wash clothes.

In 1878, when he was about 14 years old, George earned a certificate of merit from the school. He moved to Fort Scott, Kansas, and began working for a family, learning to bake bread and cook fancy meals. In Fort Scott, he went to a school that was mostly white. One night he witnessed a brutal act of racist violence.

On March 26, 1879, George was running an errand when he saw an angry group of white people beat a black man to death. They dragged the body to the village square and set it on fire. It horrified George, and he feared for his own life. He left town that night. But he never forgot the hateful act of racism as long as he lived.

SCHOOLING: School continued to be important to George. When he left Fort Scott, he traveled to Olathe, Kansas. There, he became a housekeeper for the Seymour family and attended the local high school. When the Seymours moved to Minneapolis, Kansas, George moved with them. He attended school and opened his own laundry business. Although the students at school were mostly white and George was older than most of them, he got along with everyone.

He finished high school in 1884, when he was 20 years old. It is not known if he ever received a diploma.

In the town of Minneapolis there was another person with the name of George Carver. This is when George added a "W" as his middle name so people could tell the two men apart. When someone asked him what the "W" stood for, he replied "Washington." But he never used Washington as part of his name. He was always George W. Carver.

In 1885, Carver applied by mail to Highland College, in Highland, Kansas. He was accepted, but when he arrived on campus, college officials would not let him attend because he was black. Since he had spent all his money getting there, Carver had to stay and work to save up enough money to move on.

Once again, he did laundry and cooking until he'd saved enough money. Then, he moved to Beeler, Kansas. There he worked for a farmer and saved up enough money to buy some land. He built a sod house, with a special addition. On the south side he built a room with large windows where he kept a collection of plants he gathered from the woods.

Life was hard on the farm. After four years, Carver sold his homestead for $300 and moved east to Winterset, Iowa. There, he heard about Simpson College, 25 miles away in Indianola. Carver walked all the way, arriving with almost nothing. After he paid his tuition, he had 15 cents left. He set up a laundry service and made enough money to pay for his classes.

Carver studied art and music. He was a talented artist but his art teacher, Miss Etta Budd, worried that it would be hard for an African-American man to make a living as an artist. She encour-

Carver at his graduation from Iowa State, 1894.

aged Carver to study agriculture.

Luckily, Budd's father was a professor at the Iowa State College of Agriculture and Mechanical Arts. (It's now called Iowa State University). Budd and her father helped Carver change the course of his studies. He became the first black student at Iowa State College.

COLLEGE LIFE: At college, Carver continued to face racial prejudice. Because he was black, he wasn't allowed to stay in the dormitories. He wasn't allowed to eat in the dining hall with the other students.

Somehow, he was able to overcome the prejudice and eagerly took part in many college activities. He joined the debate club, trained football players, and joined the college militia. He worked at many jobs to pay his tuition. Over the years, he worked as a janitor, waiter, and gardener in the college farms.

Carver was a good student, especially in chemistry. He continued to study art outside of class. He loved painting the plants and flowers he studied in the fields. In 1893, his sketch of the rose

Yucca gloriosa won first prize at the Columbian Exposition in Chicago.

CARVER THE TEACHER: In 1894, at the age of 30, Carver earned a Bachelor of Science degree in agriculture. He was offered a job working with a florist, but he decided to continue to study for a master's degree.

While working on his master's, Carver taught biology at Iowa State. He was also in charge of the greenhouse and worked in a lab where he studied plant diseases. He was the first African-American on the staff at Iowa State. Carver continued to make excellent drawings of plants. He completed his master's degree in agriculture in 1896.

TUSKEGEE INSTITUTE: That same year, Carver received a letter that would give him the chance to accomplish another of his goals: to improve the lives and opportunities of his fellow African-Americans.

Booker T. Washington was a former slave who had founded the Tuskegee Institute in Tuskegee, Alabama, for African-American students. Like Carver, Washington wanted to help black people improve their lives by teaching them practical skills like carpentry and farming. Washington offered Carver a job at the Institute. Carver felt the offer was his chance to make a difference. He accepted the job and became head of the agricultural department at Tuskegee.

THE SCIENCE OF FARMING: When Carver arrived in Alabama, he was struck by the poverty of the former slaves. Although they were free, they had to rent land from white farmers and grow what

Creamery operators class, Iowa State, 1894.
Carver is second from the right in the back row.

the farmers told them to grow. In Alabama, that meant cotton. Carver also noticed that the land was worn out. Even with hard work, it was impossible to make the soil yield enough crops, so the farmers could make enough money to live. Carver decided to show these new farmers how to make a good living. He wanted to teach them that science could make farming more profitable.

Word of Carver's teaching quickly spread. In his first year at Tuskegee, he had only 13 students. By the second year he had 75. Using land given by the Alabama government, Carver and his students began experiments to rebuild the worn out soil.

CROP ROTATION: Carver knew that different plants required different types of soil. He taught his students his theory of "crop rotation." By alternating, or changing the plants grown each year, the soil could be made richer and better able to produce big and healthy crops. It was a breakthrough in farming.

FINDING THE FARMERS: Carver shared his knowledge with many local farmers. But he knew there were many more who needed to learn. He decided to travel around the South to reach them. In 1906, Carver created a moveable school. He called it the Jesup Wagon, named after Morris K. Jesup, a New York banker who gave him the money to pay for the traveling school. Carver and his students began giving demonstrations to farmers on weekends. They showed them tools to help with farming and shared techniques to help them increase their crop yields.

Traveling around Alabama, Carver noticed how different the farms were from the farm where he had lived as a boy. Farmers in Alabama only grew cotton. They didn't have vegetable gardens that would give them food. Most didn't raise chickens, pigs, and cows that could provide protein.

More than 2,000 farmers a month came to see Carver's demonstrations. He encouraged them to plant vegetable gardens and showed them how to preserve meat. He also told them to take pride in their farming. He encouraged them to save a little money each day so they could one day buy their own land.

FROM COTTON TO PEANUTS: Throughout his life, Carver learned the most by paying close attention to nature. He believed that nature was the greatest teacher. His experiments focused on improving soil, finding out about plant diseases, and finding new ways to use plants.

Carver's first Faculty and Farmer's Institute, Tuskegee Institute.

While Carver was experimenting with crop rotation, he discovered that peanuts put "nutrients" back into the soil that cotton took out. In other words, if a farmer planted cotton one year and peanuts the next, the soil would stay rich. Growing peanuts also gave southern farmers another crop to sell.

At first, farmers were not interested in growing peanuts. They didn't think there was much use for them and they knew they could sell cotton. Their minds changed when the boll weevil insect appeared and destroyed entire fields of cotton. With their cotton crop ruined, they looked to peanuts.

Soon farmers had more peanuts than they could use. They fed peanuts to their animals. But there were still storehouses filled with them. The extra crop lay rotting in the fields.

Carver devoted himself to finding a way to use peanuts. In his laboratory he separated the peanut into all its parts. He found starches, oils, fats, and proteins. He then began experimenting, and discovered more than 300 products that could be made from peanuts.

OTHER DISCOVERIES: In addition to his work with peanuts, Carver used the clay soil of Alabama to create dyes. He created more than 60 products from the pecan nut and about 100 products from the common sweet potato. Studying soybeans, he discovered a crop that could be used to make many things, from oils to plastics. He also created what he called "fruit leathers" by mashing over-ripe fruit to a pulp, rolling it out like pie crust, drying it, and then cutting it into strips.

A GREAT HUMANITARIAN: Carver never got rich from his discoveries. His goal was to help farmers raise crops that would make money and give them healthy food to eat. News spread of his work and before long he became famous. He was invited to help out in nationwide efforts to increase crops, and in worldwide efforts to fight hunger.

In 1918 the U.S. government invited Carver to Washington, D.C., to discuss his discoveries. That year, U.S. troops were fighting in World War I in Europe. During the war, trade had broken off, and it was difficult to import dyes. Using American-grown products, Carver produced dyes that were used to make camouflage uniforms for soldiers. The government was also interested in his fruit leather because it was lightweight and easy to carry—perfect for soldiers. Because of the war there was also a world-wide food shortage. The U.S. government wanted to learn about the products Carver had created from sweet potatoes, peanuts, and other crops.

Thomas Edison was interested in Carver's work on producing rubber from the sweet potato. He offered him a large salary to come work in his lab in New Jersey.

Henry Ford was interested in using agricultural products in industry. This common interest led Ford and Carver to become friends. In addition, Carver was invited to speak all over the world. During the last 20 years of his life, he shared his knowledge of plants to help improve crops and fight hunger.

LAST DAYS: In March 1941, the George Washington Carver Museum was opened in Tuskegee, Alabama. Mr. and Mrs. Henry Ford were there to dedicate the collection that included plants, minerals, products made from peanuts and sweet potatoes, original paintings, and equipment from Carver's first laboratory. By this time, Carver was weak and frail.

In July 1942, Carver traveled to Dearborn, Michigan, where Henry Ford had founded Greenfield Village. In the Village, Ford had included a replica of the log cabin where Carver had lived as a child. Carver spent several weeks in Dearborn before returning to Tuskegee.

One day in December 1942, Carver suffered a serious fall. He never really recovered. On January 5, 1943, he lay down for a nap and never woke up. He is buried next to his friend, Booker T. Washington, on the Tuskegee Institute campus.

GEORGE WASHINGTON CARVER'S HOME AND FAMILY: Carver never married because, he said, he "didn't have time." He left his life earnings to the Tuskegee Institute to build a research facility where his work could be carried on after he was gone.

HIS LEGACY: During his lifetime, Carver helped thousands of southern farmers improve their lives by using his system of crop rotation. He later developed peanuts as a major crop that led to discoveries in agriculture and industry. These innovations helped fight hunger throughout the

Carver working in the lab at Tuskegee Institute.

world. Carver received many awards and honors during his lifetime. Nearly 40 years after his death, he was among the first individuals inducted into the Inventors Hall of Fame.

WORLD WIDE WEB SITES:

http://www.lib.iastate.edu/spcl/gwc/home.html
http://www.invent.org/hall_of_fame/30.html
http://www.nps.gov/gwca/expanded/auto_bio.htm

Frederick Douglass
1818 (?) - 1895
African-American Abolitionist, Editor, and Orator

FREDERICK DOUGLASS WAS BORN in Tuckahoe, in Talbot
County, Maryland, around 1818. His name when he was born was
Frederick Bailey. He was born a slave, and because of that, he
never knew his birth date. In 1845, Douglass wrote his remarkable
autobiography, *Narrative of the Life of Frederick Douglass: An American
Slave*. This powerful and important document not only relates
his life, it also records the horrible legacy of slavery in the U.S.

In his book, Douglass makes clear that most, if not all, slaves
were given no information about their birth. "By far the larger part
of the slaves know as little of their ages as horses know of theirs,

and it is the wish of most masters within my knowledge to keep their slaves thus ignorant."

Douglass also knew little about his family. He knew that his mother was named Harriet Bailey. She was a slave. His father was a white man, but Frederick never knew who he was. Frederick was taken from his mother when he was still a baby. He explains it was the "common custom" of the time, enforced by slave owners. Its goal, he says, was "to blunt and destroy the natural affection of the mother for the child."

Frederick only saw his mother four or five times in his life. She died when he was about seven years old. He was not allowed to attend her funeral.

Frederick was raised by his grandmother. He also had a brother and two sisters, but they never lived together as a family.

GROWING UP A SLAVE: Frederick had several different masters. His first master, Colonel Lloyd, owned farms and slaves in Maryland. These were controlled by an overseer (supervisor) named Plummer. Douglass described him as "a miserable drunkard, a profane swearer, a savage monster."

From a very young age, Frederick witnessed the horror and brutality of slave life. Plummer beat the slaves savagely. They weren't given enough to eat, and didn't have proper clothing. The children were given long linen shirts to wear, but not pants or shoes. They lived on cornmeal mush, which was placed in a trough on the ground. The children ate with their hands. "Few left the trough satisfied," Douglass wrote later. There were no beds. Frederick found a corn sack, and that served as his only blanket. This was his life in his earliest years.

When he was seven or eight, Frederick was sent to live with Hugh and Sophia Auld. They were relatives of Colonel Lloyd, and they lived in Baltimore. Frederick was delighted to leave the plantation. His new masters were kind to him. He was given clothing and enough food to eat. But most importantly, he learned to read.

LEARNING TO READ: Sophia Auld taught Frederick the alphabet, then how to spell simple words. When Hugh Auld found out, he made Sophia stop at once. It was against the law to teach a slave to read. Frederick soon learned another aspect of the reality of a slave's life. Keeping slaves from knowledge allowed white slave owners to keep them in their power.

Frederick determined then and there to learn to read as well as he could. "From that moment, I understood the pathway from slavery to freedom," he wrote. Baltimore was much freer than plantation life for a slave. Frederick met local boys who helped him continue to learn. They were mostly poor white children, who didn't have enough to eat. They were happy to teach Frederick to read in exchange for bread.

His reading made him determined to be free. He began to plan to escape to the North. There were fewer slaves in the North, and there were also free blacks. But most importantly, in the North there was a group of people called the **ABOLITIONISTS**. They wanted to "abolish," or end, slavery.

BACK TO THE PLANTATION: After just a few years in Baltimore, Frederick had to return to Colonel Lloyd's plantation. Lloyd had died, and Frederick had to be valued as part of the "property" of his estate, along with the horses and cattle. He was given to Lloyd's daughter, Lucretia, who sent him back to Baltimore.

BACK TO BALTIMORE: Back in Baltimore, Frederick was once again a slave owned by the Aulds. He was there for a few more years when another death in the Lloyd family made him the property of another man, Thomas Auld.

ST. MICHAEL'S: In March 1832, around the age of 14, Frederick was moved again, to St. Michael's in Maryland. Thomas Auld was "cruel and cowardly" Douglass recalled. The slaves

Sheet music cover of "The Fugitive's Song," dedicated to Douglass by the composer, Jesse Hutchinson, 1845.

were forced to work constantly, and were given little to eat or time to sleep. When he was 15, Auld "let" him to a sharecropper with a reputation for "breaking" young slaves. That is, he beat them into behaving the way he wished. But the beatings didn't break Douglass. Instead, he resolved to run away.

In 1835, he and a group of fellow slaves tried to escape. But they were betrayed, punished, and remained in slavery. Frederick was sent back to Baltimore, where he once again lived with the

Aulds. He found work in a shipyard. Yet while he made a good wage, he had to turn over every cent to Auld. This "only increased my desire to be free," Douglass wrote.

BECOMING A FREE MAN: Finally, on September 3, 1838, Frederick fled slavery. "I left my chains," he recalled, and traveled to New York. There, he was welcomed into the home of David Ruggles. He had fallen in love with a free black woman named Anna Murray. She joined him in New York, and they were married.

The couple moved to New Bedford, Massachusetts. There, the newly free Frederick gave himself a new last name: "Douglass." He worked for the first time as a free man. But the North proved to be a place of ever-present discrimination against blacks.

THE LIBERATOR: Frederick Douglass began to read a new newspaper called *The Liberator*. It was written by William Lloyd Garrison, a major abolitionist. His work was a great inspiration to Douglass. "The paper became my meat and my drink. My soul was set all on fire," he recalled.

A SPEECH ON NANTUCKET: Douglass began to speak at anti-slavery meetings. He was invited to give a talk on Nantucket on August 11, 1841. His speech was powerful and inspired the audience. Douglass was offered a job as a lecturer for the Massachusetts Anti-Slavery Society. He had found a calling he would follow for the rest of his life.

NARRATIVE OF THE LIFE OF FREDERICK DOUGLASS: Douglass was a dynamic and persuasive speaker. He was encouraged to write down his experiences, and from that came *Narrative of the Life of Frederick Douglass, An American Slave.* The book was published in 1845, when Douglass was about 28 years old.

It was the most important slave narrative ever published. Douglass spares no detail about the horrifying inhumanity of slave life. The writing is simple, powerful, and eloquent. His outrage at the state of African-Americans in bondage speaks from every line. The book was a sensation when it came out, and it made Douglass a famous man.

FLEEING TO ENGLAND: It also made him a wanted man. Douglass was still a runaway slave. There were fugitive slave laws that made it a crime to protect runaway slaves. He could be caught by slave hunters and returned to his owners. People sympathetic to slavery were outraged at what Douglass had done. They wanted him silenced.

In fear for his life, Douglass left for England. He traveled in England, Ireland, and Scotland for the next two years. There, he spoke out against slavery in the United States. The British had abolished slavery in 1834, and Douglass's speeches drew English supporters who wanted to help the cause of abolition in the U.S.

While he was in England, a few of his supporters actually purchased his freedom. That is, they raised $100 and paid it to Auld. With that act, Douglass was finally a truly free black man. He returned to the U.S. to begin the final fight against slavery.

EDITOR OF *THE NORTH STAR*: When he returned to the U.S., Douglass began to write and publish the first black newspaper in America. Called *The North Star*, the paper was published from

Douglass's home in Rochester, New York. At this time, Douglass was still a close ally of William Lloyd Garrison. But the two parted ways over an important political matter.

Garrison believed that the pro-slavery and anti-slavery states could not exist as part of the same country. Further, he saw the Constitution as a racist document that would forever deny equality to black people. Douglass grew to disagree with his mentor. He

Portrait of young Frederick Douglass

thought the Union should be preserved, and that the Constitution could be interpreted to guarantee the rights of all people, black and white. These are the principles he championed in *The North Star.*

A POWERFUL SPEAKER: Douglass delivered many important speeches in his long career. One of the most famous was "What, to the slave, is the Fourth of July?" Given on July 5, 1852, the speech outlines, with power and persuasion, the outrages of slavery. It also outlines Douglass's impassioned commitment to the cause of abolition. Here is a quote:

"I will, in the name of humanity, which is outraged, in the name of liberty, which is fettered, in the name of the Constitution and the Bible, which are disregarded and trampled upon, dare to call in question and to denounce, with all the emphasis I can command, everything that serves to perpetuate slavery—the great sin and shame of America!"

THE UNDERGROUND RAILROAD: While working as a speaker and editor for abolition, Douglass also helped in the success of the Underground Railroad. That was a network of roads and safe houses used by runaway slaves. Traveling at night, they escaped the South and found safety and freedom in the North. Rochester, New York, is on Lake Ontario, near the Canadian border. Douglass helped slaves find their way north, then across the border to safety in Canada.

WOMEN'S RIGHTS: Douglass's battle for freedom and equality extended to the rights of women. He attended the first Women's Rights Convention in Seneca Falls, New York, in 1848. He was a vibrant and vocal supporter of equal rights for all peoples.

DRED SCOTT DECISION AND THE MISSOURI COMPROMISE: In the 1850s, the specter of Civil War was evident everywhere. The people's reaction to the decision of the Supreme Court in the case of Dred Scott showed the vast divide among the American people.

The **DRED SCOTT DECISION** was handed down by the Supreme Court in 1856. The case had been brought by Dred Scott, a slave who had been taken from a Southern to a Northern state, where slavery was banned. Scott sued for his freedom, as a citizen of a free state. The Court, led by Justice Taney, ruled that "negros are deemed to have no rights which white men are bound to respect."

The Court further ruled that the Missouri Compromise was unconstitutional. That law, passed by the U.S. Congress in 1820, banned slavery in territories north and west of Missouri. The Court ruling meant that Scott, a black man, was not a citizen, and had no rights.

The decision caused a furor. "From 1856 to 1860 the whole land rocked with this great controversy," wrote Douglass.

JOHN BROWN AND THE RAID ON HARPER'S FERRY: Douglass was a friend of the fiery abolitionist John Brown. Brown did not share Douglass's belief that slavery could be ended through the political process. Instead, he believed that violence was the only way to end slavery.

Brown planned an armed insurrection, which took place at Harper's Ferry, Virginia, on October 16, 1859. There, he and his men seized the armory and held people prisoner. Brown's men were overpowered and most of them were killed. Even though he had nothing to do with the raid, Douglass became implicated in it. He had to flee to Canada and then to England. When he returned several months later, the country was on the brink of war.

THE ELECTION OF ABRAHAM LINCOLN: Abraham Lincoln was elected President in 1860. He was the candidate of the Republican Party. That party had been formed by people who were opposed to slavery in the new territories. The Southern states knew that a vote for Lincoln was a vote against slavery. Two months after the election, seven Southern states "seceded" from the Union. That means that they chose to no longer be a part of the United States. Instead, they formed their own new country, called the Confederate States of America.

CELEBRATION AT BALTIMORE ON MAY 19th 1870

THE FIFTEENTH AMENDMENT AND ITS RESULTS.

Respectfully dedicated to the colored Citizens of the U S of America A D 1870 by Schneider & Fuchs 184 N Eutaw St
Baltimore Md

Lithograph celebrating the ratification of the Fifteenth Amendment.

On April 12, 1861, Confederate soldiers fired on Fort Sumter, a fort held by Union troops in South Carolina. It was an act of rebellion. The Civil War began.

THE CIVIL WAR: The Civil War lasted from 1861 to 1865. The battles of the war were fought in several states, including Virginia, Mississippi, Pennsylvania, and Tennessee. Some of the fiercest and most decisive battles took place at Bull Run, Antietam, Chancellorsville, Vicksburg, and Gettysburg. The loss of life was terrible. All together, more than 300,000 people died in the Civil War.

AFRICAN-AMERICAN TROOPS: Douglass was a tireless advocate for the Union. He met with President Lincoln about letting black men fight for the North. Two of his sons served in the 54th Massachusetts regiment. That regiment was made up of all African-American volunteers. Their bravery was chronicled in the movie *Glory*.

THE EMANCIPATION PROCLAMATION: On January 1, 1863, Lincoln issued "The Emancipation Proclamation." It said that all slaves living in Confederate states were free. Many former slaves fled to the North, where they joined the army and fought for the Union.

Lincoln and Douglass met several times during the course of the war. They became friends and political allies. Lincoln invited Douglass to attend his second inauguration, in 1865. The war was finally coming to an end.

Tragically, Abraham Lincoln was assassinated on April 14, 1865, just five days after the Civil War ended. The nation grieved the loss of their leader. Douglass mourned the loss of a friend. First Lady Mary Todd Lincoln gave Douglass her husband's walking stick.

After the war, Douglass found his calling in the plight of the newly freed slaves who still had no guarantee of their rights. So he devoted himself to the passage of Constitutional amendments guaranteeing African-Americans their rights. Those amendments abolished slavery, made all people born in the U.S. citizens, and guaranteed blacks the right to vote.

THE THIRTEENTH AMENDMENT: For Douglass, the first important goal was to ban slavery everywhere. The Emancipation Proclamation had only freed slaves in the states that had seceded. Douglass and others fought for an amendment that abolished slavery throughout the U.S. In December 1865, the thirteenth amendment became law.

THE FOURTEENTH AMENDMENT: Next, Douglass fought for the right of full citizenship for African-Americans. The amendment that guarantees that right, the Fourteenth, was passed in 1868.

THE FIFTEENTH AMENDMENT: Douglass knew that in order to become truly free, blacks needed the right to vote. He put his powers of persuasion to work, speaking and writing about the vote. In 1870, the Fifteenth Amendment passed. It guaranteed all citizens of any race the right to vote.

THE STRUGGLE FOR WOMEN'S RIGHTS: Many women were opposed to both the Fourteenth and Fifteenth Amendments. At that time, women were not considered equal citizens. They could not vote. Douglass was a champion of women's rights, and he spoke out about it. "Right is of no Sex—Truth is of no Color," he proclaimed.

Douglass showed his devotion to the cause in the presidential election of 1872. That year, he ran for Vice President of the Equal Rights Party. The party's Presidential candidate was Victoria Claflin Woodhull. She was the first woman to run for President in the U.S.

LATER LIFE: Douglass continued to speak and write. In 1872 he moved to Washington, D.C. He became federal marshal for the District of Columbia in 1877. In 1881, he became recorder of deeds for the District.

In 1889, Douglass became minister to Haiti. He held that job for two years. He moved back to Washington, and continued to work

Portrait of Douglass taken in 1879.

for equal rights for all Americans. Frederick Douglass died on February 20, 1895, in Washington, D.C.

FREDERICK DOUGLASS'S HOME AND FAMILY: Douglass married Anna Murray in 1838, shortly after he fled to the North. They had five children. Their sons were named Lewis, Charles, and Frederick. Their daughters were named Rosetta and Annie. Annie died in 1860, and Frederick Jr. in 1892. All the other children survived their father.

Anna Douglass died in 1882. Two years later, Douglass married Helen Pitts. Some people criticized his second marriage, because Helen was white. Douglass saw it differently. He said that his first marriage honored his mother's black heritage, and his second his father's white heritage.

HIS LEGACY: Called the "Father of the Civil Rights Movement," Douglass was one of the most important advocates for freedom in history. It is hard to imagine the cause of abolition without him. He lived his early years in slavery, and chronicled its indecency in a famous memoir, bringing the truth of its horrors to the world. He helped establish the goals of the abolitionist movement. As the country headed toward Civil War, he formed alliances with political and military leaders. After the war, he used his powers of persuasion to guarantee the rights of African-Americans in the U.S. Constitution. And he lent his name to the early movement for women's rights.

A true champion of freedom, Douglass was a man whose dignity, humanity, and courage have made him a hero to generations of Americans.

WORLD WIDE WEB SITES:

http://memory.loc.gov/ammem/doughtml/doughome.html

http://www.americaslibrary.gov/cgi-bin/page.cgi/aa/douglass

http://www.cr.nps.gov/museum/exhibits/douglass

http://www.frederickdouglass.org/douglass_bio.html

http://www.history.rochester.edu/class/douglass/

http://www.nps.gov/archive/frdo/fdlife.htm

http://www.pbs.org/wgbh/aia/

W.E.B. Du Bois
1868 - 1963
African-American Historian and Civil Rights Leader

W.E.B. DU BOIS WAS BORN on February 23, 1868, in Great Barrington, Massachusetts. His full name was William Edward Burghardt Du Bois. His nickname was "Willie." His last name is pronounced "do-boys."

His parents were Mary and Alfred Du Bois. They were descended from African-American, Dutch, and French ancestors. Alfred was a barber. He left the family soon after William's birth. Mary Du Bois was a domestic worker. As a single mother, she worked hard to provide for her son.

Mary Burghardt Du Bois was also part of a large and loving family, and they helped raise Willie. They had lived in the area for more than 100 years when he was born.

W.E.B. DU BOIS GREW UP in Great Barrington as one of the only black children. Great Barrington is a rural community, in the Berkshire Mountains in western Massachusetts. Du Bois later called it "a boy's paradise." "There were mountains to climb and rivers to wade and swim and hills for coasting."

He had a happy childhood and enjoyed friends and family. But his life was touched by racism, too. He remembered being shunned by a classmate in grade school. At that time, students used to exchange cards, much as children send each other Valentine's today. One girl refused to accept Willie's card. He knew in an instant why she'd refused. It was because he was black.

"Then it dawned upon me with a certain suddenness that I was different from the others," he wrote later. He felt "shut out from their world by a vast veil." Just as quickly, he made up his mind how he'd face racism. "I had thereafter no desire to tear down that veil."

W.E.B. DU BOIS WENT TO SCHOOL at the local public schools. He was an excellent student. His mother always encouraged him to do well. His teachers recognized his talent and encouraged him, too. He worked several jobs during high school. At the age of 15, he was writing articles for newspapers in Massachusetts and New York.

Du Bois graduated from Great Barrington High at the age of 16, one year early. He was first in his class, and the only black. Sadly, his mother died just as he was getting ready for college, in 1884.

FISK: Du Bois attended Fisk University in Nashville, Tennessee, on a scholarship. Fisk is one of the finest traditional black colleges in the country. Du Bois was an excellent student. He finished his bachelor's degree in just three years. (It usually takes four.)

It was also his first experience as a black man in the South, and the difference was striking. In the summer, Du Bois taught African-American students in the Nashville area. From them, he learned the truth about life in the South for blacks. The education, housing, and job opportunities for blacks were horribly inferior. It was the world of **JIM CROW**.

JIM CROW: After the Civil War and the passage of **THE THIR- TEENTH, FOURTEENTH** and **FIFTEENTH AMENDMENTS**, black Americans thought their hard-fought, new-won rights were guaranteed. The Thirteenth Amendment banned slavery. The Fourteenth Amendment guaranteed the right of full citizenship to African-Americans. The Fifteenth Amendment guaranteed the right to vote to all male citizens, regardless of race.

RECONSTRUCTION: The term "Reconstruction" refers to the years after the Civil War when the country was rebuilding. Part of that rebuilding was political. Blacks were supposed to begin receiving their new constitutional rights.

Yet the truth of the lives of black Americans was much different. Throughout the country, particularly in the South, blacks had few if any rights. Facilities were segregated by race. Education and

*Portrait of a young African-American from the "Negro Exhibition"
created by Du Bois and presented at the Paris Exhibition, 1900.*

jobs were denied them. This is the world that Du Bois entered for
the first time as a college student.

What Du Bois witnessed changed his life. He saw that black
children were denied the basics—books, classroom materials, decent buildings. He was convinced that blacks had to fight for their
civil rights—through political, social, and educational means.

HARVARD: After completing his bachelor's degree at Fisk, Du Bois went on to graduate school at Harvard. But once again, he faced racism. Harvard didn't consider a bachelor's degree from Fisk as adequate. They made Du Bois finish another bachelor's degree. He did it, then went on to get a master's degree in history in 1891. From 1892 to 1894, he studied history at the University of Berlin, in Germany. In 1896, he received his Ph.D. in history from Harvard. He was the first black person ever to achieve a doctorate in history from the school. The topic of his doctoral thesis was the African slave trade in America.

PROFESSOR AND HISTORIAN OF AFRICAN-AMERICANS: Over the next several decades, Du Bois became a world-famous teacher, writer, and advocate for African-Americans. His first teaching job was at Wilberforce College in Ohio. He taught classics there for two years.

In 1896, Du Bois took a job at the University of Pennsylvania. There, he began the first study of a black population in the U.S. He collected data on the social, economic, and educational backgrounds of the blacks of Philadelphia.

The book he published in 1899, based on his research, was *The Philadelphia Negro*. It was a landmark work of scholarship. It influenced studies in the field for years.

THE 1900 PARIS EXHIBITION: Du Bois wanted people all over the world to know about the achievements of American blacks. In 1899, he and Daniel Murray of the Library of Congress put together an exhibit of photographs. It showcased the tremendous progress of African-Americans since the Civil War. Called "The Negro Exhibition," it opened in 1900 at the Paris Exhibition.

*23rd Annual Conference of the NAACP, Washington, D.C., May 17-22, 1932.
Du Bois is third from the right, in the front row.*

Du Bois moved on to Atlanta University, where he taught for many years. He directed studies in the scientific analysis of data about American blacks. In 1903, he published one of his most famous books, *The Souls of Black Folk*. In it, he made a prediction: "The problem of the 20th century is the problem of the color line." The remainder of his career would carry out that prediction.

BREAKING WITH BOOKER T. WASHINGTON: In the early 20th century, **Booker T. Washington** was the most important black leader in America. Washington had started the Tuskegee Institute. In an important speech in 1895, Washington had made his beliefs clear. He didn't think that American blacks should fight for voting rights, integration, or equality with whites. Instead, he favored seg-regation and a lesser, and different, status for blacks in America.

Du Bois could not support Washington's stand. The two had been friends, but Du Bois's thinking was changing. He was no longer convinced that blacks could achieve equality without fight-ing for their rights. "By every civilized and peaceful method we must strive for the rights which the world accords to men," he declared.

THE NIAGARA MOVEMENT: In 1905, Du Bois headed the Niagara Movement. It was the first all-black protest movement. He gathered like-minded people from around the country. Together, they vowed to fight for equal rights in voting, education, and jobs.

THE NAACP: Du Bois was also involved in founding the most im-portant Civil Rights organization of the 20th century, the **NAACP**. **THE NATIONAL ASSOCIATION FOR THE ADVANCEMENT OF COL-ORED PEOPLE** was formed in 1909 in response to the continuing problems of racial injustice in America.

Du Bois became the head of the NAACP's research and public-ity. He was also a member of the board of directors. (It's important to note that at its founding, the NAACP's board was mostly made up of white people. That would change in the organization's history.)

Du Bois also became the editor of the NAACP's magazine, *Crisis*. For more than 20 years, he provided a voice to the move-ment for African-American equality.

In 1934, Du Bois left the NAACP. His political ideas were changing. He began to think that integration wasn't possible. Instead, he supported African-American controlled schools and businesses. He did return, briefly, to the NAACP in the 1940s, but soon broke with the organization completely.

PAN-AFRICANISM: Du Bois had always been drawn to the movement known as "Pan-Africanism." That group advocated bringing together people of African descent from all over the world, including Africa, Asia, and North and South America. Beginning in 1900, he attended and organized Pan-African conferences.

Du Bois became an outspoken champion for world peace. He was part of the conference that founded the United Nations. In 1949, he became vice chairman of the Council on African Affairs. That group was considered anti-American by the U.S. government. Du Bois was also part of the Peace Information Center. That group wanted to ban nuclear weapons. They were also considered anti-American by the government.

In an action that has been labeled shameful and without warrant, Du Bois was charged and tried for failing to register as an agent for a foreign power. He was acquitted of all charges. Du Bois wanted to travel outside the country. But the U.S. government denied him a passport. Du Bois was furious. Finally, in 1958, he got his passport back and left the country.

Du Bois traveled throughout the world, speaking in Europe, China, and the Soviet Union. At that time, the U.S. and the Soviet Union were locked in "The Cold War." After World War II (1939-1945), the Soviet Union and the U.S. became the two strongest nations in the world. They represented two very different political systems. The U.S. was a democracy; the Soviet Union was a Communist state. The two "superpowers" also had powerful nuclear weapons. The relationship between the two nations was very important. For more than 40 years, the hostilities between these two nations affected world politics.

JOINING THE COMMUNIST PARTY: By the late 1950s, Du Bois was disillusioned with the U.S. He was discouraged by his own treatment by the government. He was also disillusioned with capitalism, the economic system of the U.S. and most of the Europe. He decided he would join the Communist Party.

"I have studied socialism and Communism long and carefully in lands where they are practiced," he wrote. "I now state by conclusion frankly and clearly: I believe in Communism. I believe that all men should be employed according to their ability and wealth and services should be distributed according to need."

These beliefs led Du Bois to become a controversial figure in America. He decided to move to Ghana, rather than to return to the U.S. There, he became director of an important project, *The Encyclopedia Africana.* He worked on it for several years.

BECOMING A CITIZEN OF GHANA: In 1963, Du Bois became a citizen of Ghana. He also renounced his U.S. citizenship. He lived in Ghana until his death, on August 27, 1963. It was the day before the historic March on Washington, D.C.

W.E.B. DU BOIS'S HOME AND FAMILY: Du Bois was married twice. He and his first wife, Nina Gomer, married in 1896. They had two children, Burghardt and Yolande. Sadly, Burghardt died when he

Portrait of Du Bois from around 1935.

was just one year old. Nina Du Bois died in 1950. Du Bois married again in 1951. His second wife was named Shirley Graham.

HIS LEGACY: Du Bois was one of the most important leaders of the movement for African-American equality. A founder of the NAACP and the most important intellectual of the movement, he refused to settle for compromise in the fight for Civil Rights. He became a controversial figure in American politics for his beliefs, as well as his membership in the Communist Party. But his commitment to the struggle for African-American rights was unquestionable.

WORLD WIDE WEB SITES:

www.americaslibrary.gov/cgi-bin/page.cgi/aa/dubois

www.duboisweb.org

www.pbs.org/wnet/jimcrow/stories_people_dubois.html

Matthew Henson
1866 - 1955
African-American Explorer
Traveled to the North Pole
with Robert E. Peary

MATTHEW HENSON WAS BORN on August 8, 1866, in Maryland. His parents were sharecroppers. They both died when he was young.

STARTING TO WORK: When he was 12, Henson walked from Washington, D.C., to Baltimore, Maryland, to find work. He was hired as a cabin boy on the ship *Katie Hines*. Captain Childs was the ship's commander. Over the next several years, he took over

Henson's education. He taught him how to sail, as well as math, geography, and other subjects.

MEETING PEARY: Henson returned to Washington around 1883. He was working in a men's store when he met Robert E. Peary. Peary was working for the Navy and planning a trip to Nicaragua. He hired Peary to be his servant, and the two left for Central America.

Peary was impressed with Henson. He told him of his plans for exploration. Henson was eager to explore, too. When Peary went on an expedition to Greenland in 1891, Henson went with him.

GREENLAND: Over the next 23 years, Peary and Henson returned to Greenland many times. In 1891, they explored the northeastern portion. They took a sledge as far as Independence Fjord to examine and map the coastline. Henson was an able navigator and dogsledder, and an excellent mechanic and carpenter.

LEARNING FROM THE INUIT: Peary and Henson met Inuit tribes and learned how they survived in the Arctic. From them, they learned the proper clothing to wear to protect against the cold. Using all of this information, Peary set his mind on his ultimate goal: the North Pole.

THE RACE FOR THE POLES: By the end of the 19th century, most of the surface of the planet had been explored. What remained were the North and South Polar regions. Explorers from many countries competed against one another to locate and claim the North Pole and South Pole. Crews from the U.S., Russia, Norway, England, Germany, and other nations were locked in a race to be the first to reach either pole.

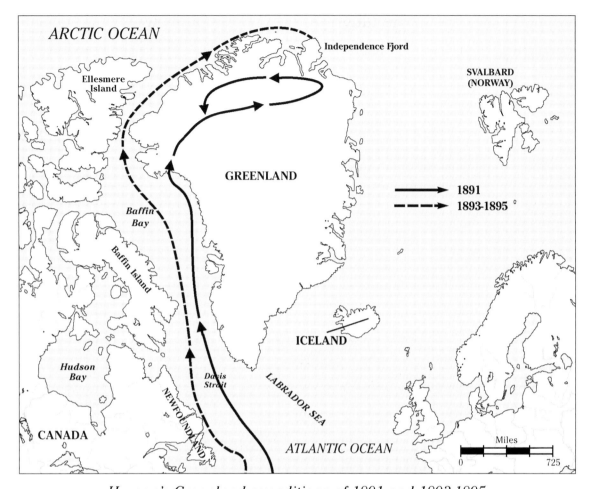

Henson's Greenland expeditions of 1891 and 1893-1895.

THE 1893-1895 EXPEDITION: Peary and Henson first attempted to reach the North Pole in 1893. That year, they traveled to northern Greenland and tried to reach the Pole. But bad weather stopped them. Throughout the next 15 years, Peary and Henson continued to attempt to reach the Pole.

THE 1905 EXPEDITION: Peary had a special boat built that could stand the ice. Aboard the *Roosevelt,* he and Henson again headed for the Pole on July 16, 1905. But the ship became stuck in the ice. The crew had to return home. They were determined to try again.

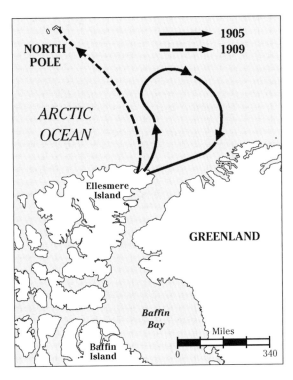

Henson's North Pole expeditions of 1905 and 1909.

REACHING THE NORTH POLE:

Their next attempt was a success. On March 1, 1909, the crew set out again from Ellesmere Island. The original team included 19 sledges and 24 men. Then, on April 6, 1909, Peary, Henson, and five Inuit reached what they thought was the North Pole. They carefully measured their location. They were confident they were the first people to reach the North Pole. They planted an American flag at the site.

COOK AND CONTROVERSY:

Peary and his crew returned to the U.S. in triumph. "We have planted the Stars and Stripes on the North Pole," he claimed. But his glory was short lived. Just before Peary made his announcement, another explorer, Dr. Frederick Cook, claimed that he had been the first to reach the Pole, in April 1908.

Peary challenged Cook's claim, as did other experts. The National Geographic Society examined all the evidence — the men's journals, maps, and calculations. They determined that Peary, not Cook, had been the first to reach the North Pole.

LIFE AFTER THE NORTH POLE EXPEDITIONS: Henson and Peary both retired from exploring after their final expedition. Henson wrote a book about his experiences. In 1913, President Taft appointed him to a job in the U.S. Customs office. He served in that job until his retirement.

Henson received many awards for his accomplishments. In 1937, he was elected to the Explorers Club of New York. He received awards from the Geographic Society of Chicago and the U.S. Department of Defense. In 1954 he was honored by President Dwight D. Eisenhower for his role in the discovery of the North Pole. A glacier in Greenland was named for him, and he received several honorary degrees. Henson died in New York City on March 9, 1955.

MATTHEW HENSON'S HOME AND FAMILY: Henson was married twice. His first marriage, to Eva Flint, ended in divorce. His second wife was named Lucy Jane Ross.

HIS LEGACY: Peary always claimed that Henson was the most valuable member of his crew. "Henson must go all the way," he said about his attempts to reach the Pole. "I can't make it there without him." Henson is buried next to Peary in Arlington National Cemetery. On his gravestone is this quote: "The lure of the Arctic is tugging at my heart. To me the trail is calling. The old trail. The trail that is always new."

WORLD WIDE WEB SITES:

http://matthewhenson.com/
http://www.unmuseum.mus.pa.us/henson.htm

Jesse Jackson
1941 -
African-American Political and
Social Activist and Leader

JESSE JACKSON WAS BORN on October 8, 1941, in Greenville, South Carolina. His name when he was born was Jesse Louis Burns. His mother was Helen Burns. She was a single teenager when Jesse was born. She didn't marry Jesse's birth father, Noah Robinson. Helen later married Charles Henry Jackson. Charles adopted Jesse, and Jesse took his last name. Helen was a hairdresser and Charles was a janitor.

JESSE JACKSON GREW UP in a family that was poor, but close. Jackson remembers what his house looked like. "Three rooms, tin-top roof, no hot or cold running water, bathroom in the backyard. Wood over the windows. Wallpaper put up not for decoration but to keep the wind out." But the family never went hungry, and they always had clothes. His parents encouraged him to do well in school, work hard, and take part in church activities.

GROWING UP IN THE SEGREGATED SOUTH: When Jackson was growing up, the South was completely segregated. Blacks couldn't go to the same schools, restaurants, movie theaters, even bathrooms as whites. "I remember begin taught my place," he recalls.

Once, when he was little, his life was threatened for forgetting that "place." He went to the local candy store, and whistled at the owner for service. The owner pulled out a gun. He threatened to shoot Jesse if he ever whistled at him again.

JESSE JACKSON WENT TO SCHOOL at the local, segregated schools. He has a vivid memory of starting school. He knew where the closest school was, right down the block. But his mom said, "That's not the one. You can't go there." Instead, they walked for blocks to the black school.

"This was it," he recalls. "The other school, the one for us. The one that didn't have any grass. They didn't plant any. Didn't mean for grass to grow here, or children to grow, either. Only place for recreation was sliding on the sand on the sidewalk. No grass to play on."

Despite the poor quality of the school facility, Jesse excelled. He was a good student and worked hard. After school he worked several part-time jobs, shining shoes, waiting tables, and cutting firewood.

Jesse went to Nicholtown School Elementary and Sterling High School. He continued to be a great student, and an athlete, too. He played basketball and baseball, and was quarterback of the state champion football team. He showed an active interest in all school activities. He was president of his class all four years, and graduated with honors in 1959.

Jackson went to the University of Illinois on an athletic scholarship. He thought he'd be playing quarterback, but faced racial discrimination immediately. Only whites were quarterbacks at Illinois. And black and white students never mixed socially. Jackson didn't like the segregation of the North any more than the South. He decided to transfer, to North Carolina Agricultural and Technical State (called "A & T").

GETTING INVOLVED IN THE CIVIL RIGHTS MOVEMENT: Jackson continued college at North Carolina A & T. The school is in Greensboro, North Carolina. There, he became involved in the Civil Rights Movement.

Students from A & T were becoming involved in a form of protest called a "sit-in." Black students would sit at segregated lunch counters that were for whites only. The owners refused to serve them, but the students wouldn't leave. They continued, day after day. Soon, the activity spread to other cities. It was an early, and effective form of protest. Lunch counters all over the South became desegregated.

Jackson with Strom Freeman, Donald Perkins, and
Martin Luther King, Jr., discussing "Operation Breadbasket," 1967.

Jackson studied sociology and economics at A & T. He was quarterback of the football team, and active in student groups. One of these groups was CORE. That was the Congress of Racial Equality. Jackson became a student leader, and led protests, marches, and sit-ins. Through these tactics, the students fought racial inequality in restaurants, stores, and other public facilities.

Jackson graduated with honors from A & T in 1964. He wasn't sure what he wanted to do next. He knew he wanted to stay involved in the struggle for Civil Rights. He thought about becoming a lawyer, then decided instead to become a minister.

BECOMING A MINISTER: Jackson went to the Chicago Theological Seminary for his studies. While living in Chicago, he continued his work for Civil Rights. He joined the Southern Christian Leadership Conference. It had been started by **Dr. Martin Luther King Jr.** It was a group of African-American ministers devoted to furthering Civil Rights. King and the SCLC believed in peaceful protest.

WORKING WITH MARTIN LUTHER KING JR.: Jackson joined King in Selma for the march for Voting Rights. He continued his religious studies, and became an ordained Baptist minister in 1968.

OPERATION BREADBASKET: By the mid-1960s, King had expanded his crusade for racial equality to the North. In Chicago, he began programs to integrate housing and employment. Jackson joined him in the efforts, especially as part of the group called Operation Breadbasket. Through boycotts and marches, they worked to help blacks find jobs.

THE DEATH OF MARTIN LUTHER KING JR.: On April 4, 1968, Martin Luther King Jr. was assassinated. Jackson was with him when he died, in Memphis, Tennessee. King was there to take part in a demonstration for sanitation workers.

King's death was a terrible blow to the Civil Rights Movement. He was considered the most important leader of the cause. Without him, the movement lost a major, unifying figure. And Jesse Jackson lost a mentor and friend.

OPERATION PUSH: In 1971, Jackson decided to leave SCLC and Operation Breadbasket. He started his own organization, Operation PUSH. The letters stand for "People United to Save Humanity." Jackson called it a "rainbow coalition of blacks and whites." Its

*Jackson leads a demonstration outside the White House
for full employment, January 15, 1975.*

purpose was to "push for a greater share of economic and political power for all poor people."

NATIONAL RAINBOW COALITION: In 1984, Jackson founded the National Rainbow Coalition. Its purpose is to fight for social justice on the national level. In 1996, Jackson merged the two organizations. It's now called the Rainbow/PUSH Coalition. The purpose of the merged organization is to fight for economic, political, and social justice.

RUNNING FOR PRESIDENT: Jackson ran for President two times, in 1984 and in 1988. He ran for the nomination of the Democratic Party. While running, he encouraged millions of Americans to register and vote. Jackson did well in the primaries leading up to the election, but lost his bid for the Party's nomination both times.

TRAVELING TO AFRICA AND THE MIDDLE EAST: Jackson has also traveled to the Middle East and other areas of conflict in the world. He considers himself an ambassador for peace. He has sometimes done this work for a particular administration. For example, in 1997, Jackson visited Kenya at the request of President Clinton to oversee free elections there. However, he does not always choose to work within the framework of any current Presidential administration. He has visited these countries to try to broker peace between fighting peoples. He has also negotiated to free Americans held as prisoners in foreign countries.

JESSE JACKSON'S HOME AND FAMILY: Jackson met Jacqueline Lavinia Brown in college. They fell in love and got married in 1963. They have five children: Santita, Jesse Jr., Jonathan, Yusef, and Jacqueline Jr.

HIS LEGACY: Jackson continues to be an important African-American leader. He works for social and political equality and to help those in need. He was active after Hurricane Katrina devastated New Orleans to get aid to the victims. He also sponsors programs to help young people, immigrants, and minorities start businesses.

WORLD WIDE WEB SITES:

http://www.pbs.org/wgbh/pages/frontline/jesse/
http://www.rainbowpush.org/about/revjackson

Mae Jemison
1956 -
African-American Scientist and Doctor
First African-American Woman to Travel in Space

MAE JEMISON WAS BORN October 17, 1956, in Decatur, Alabama. Her parents are Charlie and Dorothy Jemison. Mae's dad was a maintenance supervisor and her mom was a teacher. Mae has a sister, Ada, and a brother, Charles.

MAE JEMISON GREW UP in Chicago, where her family moved when she was four. Growing up, she had lots of friends and activities. She liked dance and sports and also loved to read and draw.

EARLY INTEREST IN SPACE: Jemison always knew she wanted to be an astronaut. She remembers watching the early space missions on TV. She knew she'd be a part of it.

"It was something I knew I wanted to do," she says. "I read lots of books about space. I don't remember the time I said, 'I want to be an astronaut'. It's just always been there."

"When I was about five or six years old, I used to look at the stars with my uncle. He would tell me they were just like the sun except they were millions of miles away. That was why they were so small. I have always been interested in astronomy and what goes on in the world. So I guess you could say I've been interested in space travel ever since I can remember."

MAE JEMISON WENT TO SCHOOL at the public schools in Chicago. The name of her grade school was Alexander Dumas Elementary School. She says she wasn't a straight-A student, although she did very well. "Maybe the reason I didn't get straight As was that I did stuff because I enjoyed it."

Jemison went on to high school at Morgan Park High. She did very well in math and science. She also enjoyed dancing and cheerleading. Jemison graduated a year early, at age 16, and went on to college.

Jemison attended Stanford University in California. She studied both engineering and African studies and graduated in 1977. Then, she went to medical school at Cornell University, getting her degree in 1981. As a medical student, she traveled to Kenya and Thailand and provided medical care to people there.

MAE JEMISON'S FIRST JOBS:
After her travels, Jemison knew she wanted to help out in poor countries. She joined the Peace Corps in 1983. That is a group that sends U.S. citizens to countries around the world to help out in many ways. Peace Corps volunteers use their skills to help people grow food, build homes, or fight disease. Jemison worked as a doctor in the African countries of Liberia (lie-BEER-ee-ah) and Sierra Leone (see-ER-uh lee-OHN) as a Peace Corps member.

Jemison holding miniature space shuttle

BECOMING AN ASTRONAUT: After two years in the Peace Corps, Jemison came back to the U.S. and began to work as a doctor. She was working in Los Angeles when she decided to apply to NASA—the National Aeronautics and Space Administration. NASA plans all the U.S. space missions and hires astronauts.

Jemison knew it might be tough to get into the space program. She was one of 2,000 people who applied to be an astronaut. Still, she wanted to fulfill her childhood dream.

In June 1987, she finally got the call she had been waiting for. She had been chosen to be an astronaut. She studied many different things to get ready to be an astronaut. She learned how to fly an airplane. She also used her training in medicine and engineering

Jemison with the crew of the Endeavor. Front row, left to right, Jerome Api and Curtis Brown; back row, N. Jan Davis, Mark C. Lee, Robert Gibson, Jemison, and Mamoru Mohri.

to understand how the body responds to space travel. As a scientist, she prepared for experiments in space.

BLAST OFF: It was five years before Jemison actually went into space. On September 12, 1992, Jemison and a crew of six blasted off. She spent eight days orbiting the Earth. While in space she studied motion sickness and took part in an experiment hatching frog eggs. Those little tadpoles became the first creatures to develop in space.

After her space flight, Jemison became famous all over the world. She was the first black woman ever to be an astronaut. Children wrote to her from all over. In Detroit, a school was named for her. The Mae C. Jemison Academy is a grade school that specializes in math and science.

In 1993, Jemison left NASA. She started her own company, The Jemison Group. Her company brings medical help and money to poor countries around the world. She also runs a science camp for kids ages 12 to 16. "The whole idea of understanding the world around you is important to everyone," she says.

Jemison continues to work to bring new technology and scientific advances to people all around the world. At her science camp, students work together to answer tough questions that affect all of us. Some of their topics have included "How Many People Can the Earth Hold" and "What To Do with All This Garbage."

MAE JEMISON'S HOME AND FAMILY: Jemison is single and lives in Houston, Texas. She has a cat named Sneeze that she got while working in Africa. She still has a lot of hobbies, including reading and dancing. She also likes to travel and she loves art. She still draws and takes photographs, and she collects African art.

HER LEGACY: Jemison is remembered as the first African-American women to travel in space. She is also known for her commitment to science, and to getting kids and other African-Americans involved in science. "I don't want kids to see me and want to be an astronaut, I want them to want to do something that's never been done. The idea is to open their imaginations."

WORLD WIDE WEB SITES:

http://starchild.gsfc.nasa.gov/docs/StarChild/whos_who_level2/
    jemison.html

http://www.princeton.edu/~mcbrown/display/jemison.html

http://www.quest.arc.nasa.gov/women/TODTWD/jemison.bio.html

Lonnie Johnson
1949 -
African-American Scientist, Inventor, and Businessman
Inventor of the Super Soaker

LONNIE JOHNSON WAS BORN on October 6, 1949, in Mobile, Alabama. He was the third of six children. Not a lot is known about his family and early years.

LONNIE JOHNSON GREW UP interested in how things worked. He loved to take things apart, then put them back together.

LONNIE JOHNSON WENT TO SCHOOL at the local public schools. He was always good at math and science. He joined the high school science club, and he took a test to see how he would do as an engineer. He didn't do too well on the test. But his mom told him not to be discouraged. "It's what you put in your head that counts," his mom said. "Nobody can take that away from you."

Johnson's whole career has proved that test wrong. As a senior in high school, he won first place in a state science fair. He had invented a robot he called "Linex." The robot was made up of parts he'd found in a junkyard. It was a remote-controlled robot, and it rolled along on wheels powered by two motors. It had a tape recorder inside, and it could talk. Johnson sent Linex commands with a walkie-talkie.

"Back then, robots were unheard of," says Johnson. "I was one of only a few kids in the country who had his own robot." Johnson was already an inventor at the age of 18.

Johnson went on to college at Tuskegee University. He studied engineering and was an excellent student. He graduated with a bachelor's degree in engineering in 1972. Johnson stayed on and earned a master's degree in engineering in 1974.

FIRST JOBS: Johnson joined the Air Force after graduation. He worked on space systems for the Air Force. While he was working there, he won many awards. He was also nominated for astronaut training.

After leaving the Air Force, Johnson worked for the Jet Propulsion Laboratory (JPL). The JPL is part of NASA—the National Aeronautic and Space Administration. Johnson didn't become an astronaut, but over the next several years, he helped build the space crafts that carried astronauts. He also designed space

Johnson with several of his Super Soakers.

probes. He worked on the Galileo probe, which has sent back valuable information about Jupiter for years. He also worked on the Mars Observer project.

While working for NASA, Johnson continued to tinker on the side. He was concerned about a problem that had troubled scientists for years. Most heating and cooling systems used in refrigerators and air conditioners used freon. Freon is a gas that contributes to pollution. Johnson wanted to build a heat pump that didn't need freon. He wanted to replace the gas with pressurized water. That's how the idea for his most popular invention came to be.

INVENTING THE SUPER SOAKER: One day in 1982, Johnson was working at home on the heat pump. By accident, he invented the Super Soaker. He hooked up the pump to the bathroom sink. Suddenly, a stream of water shot out of the nozzle. "I turned around, and it was shooting [water] across the bathroom into the tub," he recalls. "The stream of water was so powerful that the curtains were swirling in the breeze. I thought, 'This would make a great water gun'."

Johnson developed a model and his six-year-old daughter Aneka was the first to test it. She and the all the kids in the neighborhood loved it. But it would take years before the toy we now know as the Super Soaker was ready.

It took Johnson several years to work all the bugs out of his invention. He had to make sure it worked safely, so kids wouldn't hurt themselves. He had to figure out how to make it inexpensively, so kids could afford it. Finally, in 1989, he created the first Super Soaker that worked well and was affordable.

The Super Soaker is able to shoot water great distances. It can do that because of the way it's put together. The Super Soaker has a plastic container that holds the water. It also has an air pump. When the pump is pushed back and forth, it fills the container with pressurized air. When the trigger on the water gun is pressed, the air pressure forces the water out. The water shoots out fast—and far. Some Super Soakers can shoot water up to 50 feet.

Johnson visits a middle school with a new Super Soaker

Johnson applied for a patent for his invention. A patent is a government ruling that gives an inventor the right to create and sell an invention. No one else can try to duplicate the invention and sell it.

The first Super Soakers came out in the fall of 1990. Kids loved them. To date, millions have been sold. Johnson has become famous and wealthy. But he continues to tinker with his water toy. He's come out with more improvements over the years. And he's come out with several new models of the famous Super Soaker.

For the past several years, Johnson has run his own company. It's called Johnson Research and Development. In addition to the Super Soaker, Johnson works on other projects. Some are ideas for new toys, and some are serious science projects.

One important project is for the Johnson Tube. The Tube has developed from Johnson's original idea for a heat pump that worked on water instead of freon. NASA is working with Johnson to develop the Tube as a way to heat spacecraft.

Johnson has invented all kinds of things, from a wet diaper detector to hair-drying rollers to new batteries. And so far, he has more than 80 patents for his inventions.

Johnson likes to encourage young people to invent and to get involved in business. His company sets up workshops for high school students to learn how to start businesses.

LONNIE JOHNSON'S HOME AND FAMILY: Johnson lives with his wife and three children in Smyrna, Georgia. He loves the freedom his success has brought him. He especially likes spending time with his kids. And he still loves what he does. "I have these ideas," he says. "And they keep on coming."

HIS LEGACY: Johnson invented one of the most popular toys of recent times. To date, sales for Super Soakers are more than $1 billion. And Johnson continues to invent. His most recent patent is for a system that converts heat energy to electrical energy.

WORLD WIDE WEB SITES:

http://www.johnsonrd.com
http://web.mit.edu/invent/iow/johnson.html

Michael Jordan
1963 -
African-American Professional Basketball Player and Businessman

MICHAEL JORDAN WAS BORN on February 17, 1963, in Brooklyn, New York. His parents were James and Deloris Jordan. James worked in an electric plant and Deloris worked in a bank.

Michael was the youngest of five children. His brothers are James and Larry and his sisters are Deloris and Roslyn. The family moved to Wilmington, North Carolina, when Michael was seven.

MICHAEL JORDAN GREW UP in North Carolina in a busy, active family. All the kids had chores and were encouraged to work hard. Michael's mom taught him to wash clothes, cook, clean the house, and sew. All the kids were expected to do well in school and to stay out of trouble.

Michael loved sports as a child. He played basketball and football, but his favorite sport was baseball. He remembers being named most valuable player on his baseball team. "That was the first big thing I accomplished in my life," he says.

MICHAEL JORDAN WENT TO SCHOOL at the public schools in North Carolina. He didn't always do well in school. In fact, he spent more time playing sports than he did studying. When he was in high school, he got suspended three times for bad grades. His dad told him that if he didn't study harder and get better grades, he wouldn't be able to go to college.

Jordan knew it was important to get into college. By the time he was in high school, he had become a basketball superstar. He wanted to go to a good school and play college ball. He also wanted to play in the NBA (National Basketball Association).

Jordan knew he had to do well in school to achieve his goal of playing pro basketball. So he buckled down and studied. When he graduated from high school in 1981, many colleges wanted him to come to their school. He chose the University of North Carolina, a school with a great basketball team.

PLAYING COLLEGE BASKETBALL: Jordan played on the North Carolina team for three years. The team had a great record during Jordan's years. In his first year, he helped the team to win the college championship in basketball. In his second and third years, he was named Player of the Year.

After three years in college, Jordan decided to leave school and join the NBA. He wanted to play professional basketball at that point in his life. (He did finish his college degree in 1986, after he had turned pro.)

LIFE AS A PROFESSIONAL BASKETBALL PLAYER: In 1984, Jordan was chosen in the first round of the draft by the Chicago Bulls of the NBA.

When Jordan joined the team, they were not the World Champions. In fact, they were doing very badly. Jordan helped to change that. In his first year, he played terrific basketball. Fans loved the

Jordan heads toward the basket, showing his incredible jumping ability.

new player who could sail through the air and score. Jordan was named "Rookie of the Year" that year.

1984 OLYMPICS: In 1984 Jordan also played on the U.S. Olympic team. The team won a Gold Medal for first place in basketball.

BACK TO THE BULLS: Jordan returned to the Bulls after the Olympics. In his second year in the NBA, he injured his foot. He had to miss a lot of games. But when he was better, he and the Bulls came roaring back.

During his third season, Jordan became the second player in history to score over 3,000 points. It was the highest single-season scoring record for a guard (his position). In the 1987-89 season, Jordan racked up some incredible statistics. He was named NBA Defensive Player of the Year and MVP. By 1990, the team was in the conference finals, led by their star. They were defeated in their drive for an NBA Championship by the Detroit Pistons, but that was the last time that would happen for a while.

In 1991, 1992, and 1993, Jordan led the Bulls to three straight NBA Championships. He began to be known as the best basketball player ever. He has won the major awards in the game many times. He has been named Most Valuable Player (MVP) in the NBA five times. He has also been named the MVP of the NBA finals four times.

1992 OLYMPICS: In 1992, Jordan appeared again in the Olympics. This time, he was part of a group of players known as the "Dream Team." The team included Magic Johnson, Charles Barkley, David Robinson, Isaiah Thomas, and other NBA stars. They were an awesome team, probably the best ever to play in the Olympics. Jordan and the team won another Gold Medal for the U.S.

SWITCHING TO BASEBALL: In October 1993, Jordan shocked many sports fans when he decided to retire from basketball. He said he had always wanted to play pro baseball. So he started to play with the Chicago White Sox farm team.

It was a difficult time in Jordan's life. His father was killed in the summer of 1993. Jordan had to deal with the loss of his father and the constant attention of news reporters interested in the case of his father's death.

Jordan played baseball for just over one year. Then he decided he would return to basketball. He went back to his old team, the Chicago Bulls, in the middle of the season.

RETURNING TO THE BULLS: When Jordan returned to the Bulls in 1995, he was a little rusty. But fans all over the world welcomed back the man many consider the greatest player ever. The team didn't get very far in the playoffs that season, but Jordan improved with every game. By 1996, the team was back, and Jordan was in great form.

Jordan and the Bulls dominated the 1995-96 basketball season. They went all the way to the finals with the most wins ever for a team in the NBA. Jordan loved being back, and he loved winning another NBA crown.

The 1996-97 saw Jordan and the Bulls back in the championships. They won the NBA championship again, with Jordan

Jordan, right, at his annual Celebrity Invitational golf tournament.

showing as much power as ever. It was a "three-peat" for the Bulls in 1997-98, as they once again captured the NBA title.

Jordan's playing style was known to his millions of fans. He leapt into the air and just seemed to hang there on his way to the basket. He could score as many as 50 points in a game. Often when he went into the basket, his tongue hung out of his mouth. He concentrated so hard, he didn't even realize he was doing it.

ANOTHER RETIREMENT, AND ANOTHER COMEBACK: Jordan retired from basketball in 1998 after leading the Chicago Bulls to their sixth NBA title in 10 years. But in 2001 he decided he wanted to play again, this time for the Washington Wizards. He was already president of the team, but he decided that even though he was 38, he wanted to play. "I am returning as a player to the game I love," Jordan said. He also donated his first year's salary to the victims of the September 11 terrorist attacks on the U.S.

Jordan played one more year in the NBA. The 2002-03 season was his last, and he gave it his all. He surpassed Wilt Chamberlain on the all-time scoring list, making it to third place, with 31,420 career points. He was the only Wizard to play every single game that season.

LIFE AFTER BASKETBALL: Jordan has been involved with several businesses over the years. He is part owner of the Charlotte Bobcats, an NBA expansion team. He appears in ads for his famous "Air Jordan" shoes and other products. He also owns several restaurants.

Jordan is involved with many charities that help out kids. He built a Boys and Girls Club in Chicago in honor of his dad. He gives to the Ronald McDonald Children's Charities, the Make-a-Wish Foundation, the Special Olympics, the United Negro College Fund, and others. Through Nike, he's started a program called the Breakfast Club. It's aimed at helping kids dedicate themselves to hard work and excellence in life. He's also traveled the world bringing sports to kids. In 2006, he toured Europe and ran camps for young athletes.

Jordan loves to play golf, and has turned his talent at that sport to charity, too. He hosts a celebrity golf tournament that raises money every year for good causes. In 2005, he donated the proceeds to the Red Cross, to help victims of the tsunami in Asia.

MICHAEL JORDAN'S HOME AND FAMILY: Michael Jordan married his wife Juanita in 1989. They have two sons, Jeffrey and Marcus, and a daughter, Jasmine. The couple divorced in 2007. They share joint custody of their children.

HIS LEGACY: Jordan is considered by many to be the finest basketball player in history. His honors and awards are astounding. He won two Olympic Gold Medals and holds many NBA records for scoring. He's also known as a generous contributor to many charities and organizations that help kids be their best.

WORLD WIDE WEB SITES:

http://www.nba.com/playerfile/michael_jordan/
http://www.23jordan.com/bio1.htm

Jackie Joyner-Kersee
1962 -
African-American Athlete, Activist, and Olympic Gold Medalist
Named Greatest Female Athlete of the 20th Century

JACKIE JOYNER-KERSEE WAS BORN March 3, 1962, in East St. Louis, Illinois. Her parents were Alfred and Mary Joyner. Jackie is the second of four children. She has an older brother named Al and two younger sisters named Angela and Debra.

Jackie was named by her grandmother for Jacqueline Kennedy. She was the wife of President John Kennedy and the First Lady.

Jackie Joyner's grandmother said that little Jackie was sure to "be first lady of something" when she grew up.

JACKIE JOYNER-KERSEE GREW UP in East St. Louis in a poor, rough neighborhood. The Joyner family was poor. Jackie's father worked for the railroad and didn't make much money. Her mother worked as a nurse's assistant, and she didn't make much, either. Sometimes the family had only mayonnaise sandwiches to eat. Sometimes they couldn't afford to pay for heat, and they slept around the stove to keep warm.

Even though they were poor, the Joyners raised their kids to have strong values. They expected their children to do well in school and to treat everyone with respect. And they taught their children the importance of family.

JACKIE JOYNER-KERSEE'S EARLY LIFE: Jackie's house was near a youth center and she spent a lot of time there. She wanted to take part in the track and field games at the center. A local coach named Nino Fennoy gave Jackie a lot of encouragement. She told him she wanted to compete, and he helped her to become one of the greatest athletes of all time.

Coach Fennoy remembered how hard she worked and how much she loved to race. When she ran her first race, she finished last. But she wasn't discouraged. She had a big smile on her face. Coach Fennoy remembered "her pigtails, the little skinny legs, the knees, and smile."

Within a short time, Jackie was showing the determination and willingness to work hard that made her a champion. Soon, she was winning all her races. Her little sisters helped out, too. They

Jackie around age 10.

brought sand into the Joyner backyard in potato chip bags to make Jackie a sand pit for long jump practice. She began to compete in the pentathlon. That's a five-event competition that includes running, jumping, and hurdles. By the time she was 14, she was National Junior Pentathlon Champion. She won the title for four years straight.

JACKIE JOYNER-KERSEE WENT TO SCHOOL at the public schools in East St. Louis. She always did well in school, and she was great in sports. She also took dance and acting classes and was a cheerleader. At Lincoln High School, she was a star of the basketball and volleyball teams. After high school, she went to the University of California at Los Angeles, called UCLA.

During her first year of college, Jackie's mother got very sick and died. Jackie had a very hard time dealing with her mother's death. She was training with a new coach, Bob Kersee. Bob had also lost his mother when he was a teenager. He gave Jackie support and understanding. As he helped her get over her sadness, Bob also helped her to focus on her school work and sports. They fell in love, and married in 1986.

Jackie went on to have a terrific college sports career. She was named Most Valuable Player (MVP) of the basketball and track teams. She graduated with a degree in history in 1986.

ASTHMA: In the 1980s, Jackie discovered she had exercise-induced asthma. The disease causes the air pathways in the lungs to swell and prevent breathing. It can even be fatal. Jackie continued to battle asthma throughout her career. But she refused to let it ruin her chance to become an athletic champion.

BECOMING A GREAT ATHLETE: Jackie competed in a very tough event called the "heptathlon" (hep-TATH-lon). It is made up of seven different events. They are the 200-meter run, the 100-meter hurdles, the high jump, the long jump, the shot put, the javelin throw, and the 800-meter run. The athlete with the highest combined score for these events is the winner.

OLYMPIC AND WORLD TITLES: In 1984, Joyner-Kersee made the Olympic team in the heptathlon. It was a dream come true for her. Even though she had trained hard and many people thought she would place first, Joyner-Kersee had an injury just before the Olympics. She placed second, winning the silver medal.

In 1988, Jackie competed again in the heptathlon at the Olympics. This time, she won two gold medals: one in the heptathlon and another in the long jump. She continued to train and compete. In addition to the Olympics, she also competed in national and world championships. She won championships and broke records all over the world. She still holds the World Record for total accumulated points in the heptathlon.

In the 1992 Olympics, Jackie won another gold medal in the heptathlon. She also won a bronze medal in the long jump. Joyner-Kersee kept training, with her eyes on what would be her final Olympics, in 1996. Sadly, she had to withdraw from the heptathlon because of an injured thigh. But she wouldn't give up. She competed in the long jump that year, and through sheer determination, she won a bronze. All together, she has six Olympic medals, won in four Olympics.

In 1998, Joyner-Kersee competed in her final meet. At the Goodwill Games, she finished her last heptathlon, and she went out in style, with a first-place finish. "I can't believe it's over," she said. "I can't believe the time went so quickly."

Joyner-Kersee competes in the high jump for UCLA, 1986.

Joyner-Kersee's track accomplishments are incredible. But she was also a fine basketball player. In college, she was an all-conference player for UCLA. And after she'd retired from track in 1996, she played for the women's team in Richmond.

A ROLE MODEL FOR A GENERATION: This quiet, modest woman's achievements spoke volumes to an entire generation of young girls. Soccer great Mia Hamm was only 12 when she watched Joyner-Kersee competing in her first Olympics. What impressed Hamm wasn't her silver medal, but her determination and spirit. "You could see that she loved everything she did and that she invested every ounce of strength she had in it," Hamm recalls. "You saw her and you got the idea of what a woman athlete should be. At the time it seemed almost like she wasn't responsible for just her sport, but for all women's sports."

LIFE AFTER SPORTS: Joyner-Kersee is retired from sports, but busier than ever. She runs a sports marketing business and a sports medicine business. She also devotes her time to her foundation, the Jackie Joyner-Kersee Foundation, based in East St. Louis.

She opened the Jackie Joyner-Kersee Center in East St. Louis in 2000. The Center is a community resource used by thousands of residents each year. It's a place where they can come together to learn and to play. There's classes for everybody, from kids to seniors. Jackie suffers from asthma, so she's made asthma awareness and healthy lifestyles a priority for the center.

JACKIE JOYNER-KERSEE'S HOME AND FAMILY: Jackie married her coach, Bob Kersee, in 1986. They live in East St. Louis. Jackie's still close to her family, including brother Al, who was an Olympic champion and coach. He was married to the late track champion Florence Griffith-Joyner.

HER LEGACY: Jackie Joyner-Kersee is considered by many to be the finest female athlete ever. In 2000, *Sports Illustrated for Women* named her the "Greatest Female Athlete of the 20th Century." This is what they said about her: "In every revolution there is a leader. Whether vocal or silent, whether by purpose or happenstance, there is a figure whose shadow falls across an era and whose footprints mark the path for others to follow. In ways that could be measured, Jackie Joyner-Kersee was one of the greatest Olympic

Joyner-Kersee competes in the long jump
at the 1996 Olympics.

athletes in history. And in ways that could not, she was a rare combination of courage and grace."

Always humble, Joyner-Kersee sums up her contribution this way: "I realize that I've been blessed to do well in athletics. And I have had a lot of opportunities and a lot of doors have been opened for me. I think being able to share that with someone else is a great satisfaction like winning the gold, being able to give back."

WORLD WIDE WEB SITES:

http://www.jackiejoyner-kerseefoundation.org

http://sportsillustrated.cnn.com/sifor women/top_100/1/

http://www.espn.go.com/sportscentury/features/

Coretta Scott King
1927 - 2006
African-American Civil Rights Leader

CORETTA SCOTT KING WAS BORN on April 27, 1927, in Heiberger, Alabama. Her parents were Bernice and Obadiah Scott. They were farmers. Obadiah also ran a country store and worked as a barber. Bernice drove a school bus. Coretta was one of three children. She had an older sister named Edythe and a younger brother named Obie.

CORETTA SCOTT KING GREW UP in a poor, hardworking family. Coretta and the other children worked on the farm, picking cotton and taking care of the animals and the garden.

GROWING UP BLACK IN THE SEGREGATED SOUTH—JIM CROW:
Coretta grew up at a time when black people did not have the same rights as white people. Blacks could not buy houses or find jobs where they wanted. In the South, they couldn't use the same buildings as white people. Blacks had to use different restaurants, movie theaters, even drinking fountains. They went to segregated schools.

CORETTA SCOTT KING WENT TO SCHOOL at a one-room public school for black children. It was five miles away from her home. There were no buses for black children; she walked all the way. Most days, the bus for white children, whose school was much closer to her house, would pass her on her walk. It was the kind of injustice she, and all blacks, lived with every day.

Coretta was an excellent student. She was also an outstanding musician. She could play piano, and had a beautiful singing voice. For high school, she attended the private Lincoln School. She graduated first in her class in 1945.

Coretta went on to Antioch College in Ohio, on a full scholarship. She majored in music and education. She graduated from Antioch in 1949. She continued to study music at the New England Conservatory in Boston. That's one of the finest music schools in the country. It was while studying there that she met Martin Luther King Jr.

GETTING INVOLVED IN THE CIVIL RIGHTS MOVEMENT: By the time she was in college, Coretta Scott had become involved in the Civil Rights Movement. People in the movement fought for equal rights for blacks. They wanted equal education, health care, housing, and jobs. She joined groups like the **NAACP (NATIONAL**

Coretta Scott King and husband, Martin Luther King, Jr.,
sit with three of their four children—Martin III, Dexter, and Yolanda—
in their Atlanta, Ga. home, on March 17, 1963.

ASSOCIATION FOR THE ADVANCEMENT OF COLORED PEOPLE)
who were fighting for freedom.

DR. MARTIN LUTHER KING JR.: When Coretta Scott met Martin
Luther King Jr., he was studying for his Ph.D. in theology. That's
the study of religion. They fell in love and married in 1953. After

that, they moved to Montgomery, Alabama. There, Dr. King became minister of the Dexter Avenue Baptist Church.

King was deeply committed to the fight for Civil Rights. His focus was simple and clear. He believed that it was only through nonviolent demonstrations that equality for blacks could be won. He also fought for peace and the end of poverty for all people. He was already emerging as a major leader in the movement when he married Coretta.

THE MONTGOMERY BUS BOYCOTT: In 1955, a courageous woman named **Rosa Parks** refused to give up her seat in the "whites only" section of a Montgomery bus. She was arrested for refusing to give up her seat. That led to a famous action of the Civil Rights movement.

Parks challenged her arrest in court. Civil Rights groups used her case to plan the Montgomery Bus Boycott. They asked black people not to ride the buses in Montgomery until the laws were changed.

One of the leaders of the boycott was Dr. Martin Luther King Jr. He was arrested and sent to jail for his work on the boycott. Yet through his actions, people all over the country, and the world, could see how unfair the segregation laws were.

The boycott changed the laws in the U.S. It led to a Supreme Court ruling in 1956 outlawing segregation on buses. The movement for Civil Rights had won a great victory. But there was still much to do.

Over the next decade, Coretta Scott King actively worked with her husband in the movement. She had many other duties besides,

Coretta Scott King and her husband, Dr. Martin Luther King, Jr.,
marching for voting rights for blacks,
Montgomery, Alabama, on March 25, 1965.

including raising the couple's four children. But she remained devoted to Civil Rights.

She said that, at first, Dr. King had a more "traditional" view of women. "He'd say, 'I have no choice, I have to do this, but you haven't been called.' And I said, 'Can't you understand? You know I have an urge to serve just like you have'."

Yet he did understand, and value, his wife's commitment. "I wish I could say, to satisfy my male ego, that I led her down this path," King said. "But I must say we went down together. She was as actively involved and concerned when we met as she is now."

During these years, Coretta Scott King also planned and produced Freedom Concerts. These were fund raisers, in which she would read and sing, spreading the word of Civil Rights.

But fighting for equality was dangerous work. The Kings' lives were threatened. Their home was firebombed. They faced violence and racial hatred. That hatred led to Dr. King's death.

THE ASSASSINATION OF MARTIN LUTHER KING: Dr. Martin Luther King Jr. was shot to death on April 4, 1968, in Memphis, Tennessee. It was a devastating loss, for Coretta Scott King as a wife and mother. For the nation, it meant the passing of perhaps the most important Civil Rights leader in history.

CONTINUING THE FIGHT FOR CIVIL RIGHTS: Coretta Scott King showed her courage and her commitment to her husband's legacy immediately. Dr. King had gone to Memphis to take part in a march for justice for sanitation workers. Coretta marched with the workers, as plans went on for her husband's funeral.

That set the tone for the rest of her life. For the next 38 years, she devoted herself to keeping the fight for Civil Rights alive. She fought for legislation to end discrimination. She fought against injustice everywhere, in the U.S. and abroad. She fought against poverty, violence, and for the rights of women and children. She became an outspoken critic of the racist system in South Africa.

Most importantly, King dedicated her life to two important goals. She wanted the country to create a national holiday in honor of her husband. And she wanted to create a center built in his honor. She managed to complete both.

THE MARTIN LUTHER KING JR. HOLIDAY: In 1983, after 15 years of work, Coretta Scott King accomplished one of her goals. Congress approved a law making the third Monday in January "Martin

*Coretta Scott King speaking at the commemoration of her husband
Martin Luther King, Jr.'s "I Have a Dream" speech in 2003.*

Luther King Jr. Day." It is a federal holiday. Each year, people
around the country celebrate the life and work of this great man.

THE KING CENTER: Coretta Scott King also worked for nearly 30
years to build the King Center. It is a 23-acre national historic park
in Atlanta, Georgia. It includes Dr. King's tomb, a library, museum,
and exhibits devoted to education and history. It is also a center
for study and learning about Dr. King's life and the movement for
Civil Rights. A few years ago, Coretta turned the direction of the
center over to her son Dexter.

CORETTA SCOTT KING'S HOME AND FAMILY: Coretta Scott married Martin Luther King, Jr. on June 18, 1953. They had four
children, Yolanda, Martin III, Dexter, and Bernice.

King suffered a stroke and heart attack in August 2005. She also had cancer. In January 2006, she went to Mexico for treatment. She died there on January 30, 2006. She was 78 years old.

HER LEGACY: At the time of her death, tributes to this courageous Civil Rights leader poured in from all over the world. "She wore her grief with grace. She exerted her leadership with dignity," said the Reverend Joseph Lowery. "She was a woman born to struggle," said Andrew Young. "She has struggled and she has overcome."

WORLD WIDE WEB SITES:

http://www.achievement.org/
http://www.npr.org/
http://www/kingcenter.org/csk/bio.html

Martin Luther King Jr.
1929 - 1968
African-American Civil Rights Leader
and Religious Leader
Winner of the Nobel Prize for Peace

MARTIN LUTHER KING JR. WAS BORN on January 15, 1929, in Atlanta, Georgia. His name when he was born was Michael, but he later changed it to Martin. His parents were Alberta and Martin Luther King Sr. Alberta was a homemaker. Martin Sr. was a minister, as was his father. Martin Jr. had an older sister named Christine and a younger brother named Alfred.

MARTIN LUTHER KING JR. GREW UP in Atlanta in a loving family that was devoted to service and faith.

MARTIN LUTHER KING JR. WENT TO SCHOOL at local, segregated schools in Atlanta. He went to school for the first time at the age of five. At that time, the legal age to enter school was six. So when the school officials found out his real age, he had to wait a year to start again.

Martin attended Younge Street Elementary and David T. Howard Elementary Schools. He was always an outstanding student. He went on to Atlanta University Laboratory School and Booker T. Washington High School. When he was a junior in high school, he took college exams that showed how advanced he was. He was able to go to college at 15, skipping two years of high school.

King went to Morehouse College. That's one of the finest traditional black colleges in the country. It's also a school for men only. At Morehouse, he studied sociology. He received his bachelor's degree from Morehouse in 1948.

By that time, King was thinking about becoming a minister, like his father and grandfather. He decided to go to Crozer Theological Seminary in Chester, Pennsylvania. He studied theology at Crozer for three years. Once again, he was an outstanding student. He won awards and scholarships, and was president of his class. He received his bachelor of divinity degree in 1951.

King decided he wanted to continue to study religion. In the fall of 1951, he started working on his doctoral degree in theology at Boston University. In Boston, he met a student named **Coretta Scott**. She was studying music at the New England Conservatory. They fell in love, and married in 1953. She would be his partner in the struggle for **CIVIL RIGHTS** for the next 15 years.

JOINING THE DEXTER AVENUE BAPTIST CHURCH: King received his Doctor of Divinity degree in 1955. He moved to Montgomery, Alabama, where he became the pastor of the Dexter Avenue Baptist Church. He and Coretta became involved with the **NAACP. THE NATIONAL ASSOCIATION FOR THE ADVANCEMENT OF COLORED PEOPLE** was one of the most important organizations of the Civil Rights movement. It was a momentous time for him, and for the struggle for Civil Rights.

GETTING INVOLVED IN THE CIVIL RIGHTS MOVEMENT: It was in Montgomery that King became a giant of the Civil Rights movement. It started with the defiance of a woman named **Rosa Parks.**

At that time, blacks could not sit in the same section of the bus as whites. A black person had to enter a bus at the front and pay the fare. Then they had to get out of the bus and get back in at the back. Parks rode the bus to work each day in Montgomery. Each day she had to sit in an area for blacks only.

THE MONTGOMERY BUS BOYCOTT: Rosa Parks became a hero for challenging the laws that kept blacks from being equal. It happened on a bus in Montgomery on December 1, 1955. On that day, Parks took a seat in the first row of the "blacks only" section of the bus. A white man got on and found that all the seats in the white section were taken. The bus driver told the people in Rosa's row to stand and give their seats to the white man. Park's wouldn't do it.

"I had had enough," she recalls. "I wanted to be treated like a human being." The driver told her she had to move. She wouldn't. He said he would call the police. She told him to go ahead. Rosa Parks was arrested that day for refusing to give her seat on the bus to a white man.

King makes his famous "I Have a Dream" speech
at the Lincoln Memorial in Washington, D.C., August 28, 1963.

Black Civil Rights leaders asked Parks to challenge the law that allowed her to be arrested. She agreed, even though she knew she would be in danger. Civil Rights groups used her case to plan the Montgomery Bus Boycott. King was elected president of the Montgomery Improvement Association. They asked black people not to ride the buses in Montgomery until the laws were changed.

It was a great sacrifice for most of the blacks in Montgomery. Many were poor and needed the bus to get to work. But they stood behind Parks, King, and the Civil Rights leaders. Almost all the blacks "boycotted," or did not use, the buses.

People all over the country became involved in the Montgomery Bus Boycott. They organized, raised money, and let people all over the country know how unfair the laws were. Some people, including King, were arrested and sent to jail for their work on the boycott. His home was firebombed, and he received threats against his safety.

The boycott lasted a year, and King became the face of the boycott and the movement. In December 1956, the U.S. Supreme Court declared that Alabama's segregated bus system was unconstitutional. It was a great triumph for the Civil Rights movement.

SOUTHERN CHRISTIAN LEADERSHIP CONFERENCE: In 1957, King helped found the Southern Christian Leadership Conference (SCLC). It was a group of African-American ministers devoted to furthering Civil Rights. King and the SCLC believed in peaceful protest. In that, they were following the teachings of their Christian faith.

GANDHI: In 1959, King toured India. He had always been drawn to the nonviolent philosophy of the Indian leader Mohandas Gandhi. Gandhi had shown, through his own political protests in India, how effective nonviolence could be in changing society. King studied Gandhi's methods, and returned to the U.S. with renewed energy.

Over the next several years, King traveled the world, speaking on behalf of Civil Rights. He also took part in demonstrations, bringing the plight of black people to light. In the early 1960s, groups of college students began to stage "sit-ins," trying to desegregate public places, such as restaurants. Often, these young people were harassed and beaten. In the South, the fight for integration was especially violent.

BIRMINGHAM, ALABAMA: In 1963, King organized large demonstrations in Birmingham, Alabama. The demonstrators were protesting the segregation of schools, stores, and restaurants. They were also protesting the treatment of local police, who were known for their brutal tactics. By this time, King was a well-known leader. The demonstrations he led were followed by the media from all over the world.

In one incident, Birmingham police turned fire hoses and attack dogs on unarmed protesters. The shameful scene was flashed on televisions the world over. Americans were outraged at the violence and hatred of the police.

LETTER FROM A BIRMINGHAM JAIL: During the demonstrations, King was arrested for demonstrating without a permit. He spent 11 days in jail. While there, he wrote a famous document, "Letter from a Birmingham Jail." In it, he outlined the purpose and means of the Civil Rights movement.

"I am in Birmingham because injustice is here," he wrote. "Injustice anywhere is a threat to justice everywhere."

The response to the Birmingham protests was swift. By May 10, 1963, the stores, schools, and restaurants of the city were desegregated. President John F. Kennedy submitted Civil Rights legislation to Congress. King had shown that nonviolence worked.

King escorts black children to formerly all-white schools in Grenada, Mississippi, Sept. 20, 1966.

THE MARCH ON WASHINGTON: In August 1963, the largest civil rights demonstration in the nation's history took place. Nearly 250,000 demonstrators came to Washington, D.C. They heard one of the most famous speeches in history, from Dr. Martin Luther King Jr.

"I HAVE A DREAM": On the steps of the Lincoln Memorial, King spoke to the protesters, and to all the world. His words echo down the years, inspiring new generations.

"I have a dream that one day this nation will rise up and live out the true meaning of its creed. 'We hold these truths to be self-evident, that all men are created equal.' I have a dream that one day on the red hills of Georgia, sons of former slaves and the sons of former slave-owners will be able to sit down together at the table of brotherhood.

"I have a dream that my four children will one day live in a nation where they will not be judged by the color of their skin, but by the content of their character.

"From every mountainside, let freedom ring. And when we allow freedom to ring—when we let it ring from every village and every hamlet, from every state and every city, we will be able to speed up that day when all of God's children, black men and white men, Jews and Gentiles, Protestants and Catholics, will be able to join hands and sing in

King receiving the Nobel Peace Prize from Gunnar Jahn, Dec. 10, 1964.

the words of the old Negro spiritual: Free at last, free at last. Thank God almighty, we are free at last."

THE NOBEL PRIZE: In 1964, King was awarded the Nobel Prize for Peace. That is one of the most important honors in the world. It meant that he was recognized not just in the U.S., but around the world, as a peacemaker. Just 35 years old, King was the youngest person ever to receive the award.

Once again, King made a notable speech. He said, in part:

"I accept this award today with an abiding faith in America and an audacious faith in the future of mankind. I refuse to accept the view that mankind is so tragically bound to the starless midnight of racism and war that the bright daybreak of peace and brother-hood can never become a reality."

In 1964, King was named *Time* magazine's "Man of the Year" award. He also was present at the signing of the landmark **CIVIL RIGHTS ACT**. But King knew there was still work to do.

VOTING RIGHTS—THE MARCH FROM SELMA TO MONT-GOMERY: In 1965, King organized demonstrations for voting rights. In many areas of the country, black people were prevented from registering to vote. They were forced to take ridiculous tests. Some were threatened if they even tried to register.

King led demonstrations in Selma, Alabama, to secure voting rights for all people. The protesters were met with clubs, cattle prods, and tear gas. Americans watched in horror as the protesters were beaten. King put out the call for volunteers. More than 50,000 Americans joined in the march. Their efforts led to the Voting Rights Act of 1965, which guaranteed all Americans, regardless of race, the right to vote.

ENDING PREJUDICE, POVERTY, AND WAR: In the mid-1960s, King continued the battle for Civil Rights. He started a campaign in Chicago to fight for equality in housing, schools, and jobs. He also extended his vision of America to include all poor people. He began a Poor People's Campaign that embraced the poor of all races.

King also spoke out against the war in Vietnam. He did not be-lieve it was a just war. He met with President Lyndon Johnson, who had been a staunch supporter of Civil Rights. They didn't agree, but King made his opinions clear to the President.

KING'S FINAL DEMONSTRATION: On April 3, King arrived in Memphis, Tennessee, to support striking sanitation workers. Once again, he gave a heartfelt and rousing speech to the workers.

"Let us rise up tonight with a greater readiness. Let us stand with a greater determination. And let us move on in these powerful days, these days of challenge to make America what it ought to be.

"Well, I don't know what will happen now. We've got some difficult days ahead. But it really doesn't matter with me now, because I've been to the mountaintop and I don't mind. Like anybody, I would like to live a long life. But I'm not concerned about that now. I just want to do God's will, and He's allowed me to go up to the mountain. And I've looked over and I've seen the Promised Land. I may not get there with you, but I want you to know tonight, that we as a people will get to the Promised Land. And I'm happy tonight. I'm not worried about anything. I'm not fearing any man. Mine eyes have seen the glory of the coming of the Lord."

ASSASSINATION: The next day, April 4, 1968, King was assassinated. He was shot while standing on the balcony of his motel room. The nation was shocked. Riots broke out in cities all over the country. His funeral was attended by thousands, and watched by millions.

The man who shot King was named James Earl Ray. He was caught, convicted, and sentenced to 99 years in jail.

King confers with President Lyndon Johnson in the Oval Office, 1966.

After King's death, his wife, **Coretta Scott King,** dedicated her life to continuing his goals. She wanted the country to create a national holiday in honor of her husband. And she wanted to create a center built in his honor. She managed to complete both.

THE MARTIN LUTHER KING JR. HOLIDAY: In 1983, after 15 years of work, Coretta Scott King accomplished her first goal. Congress approved a law making the third Monday in January "Martin Luther King Jr. Day." It is a federal holiday. Each year, people around the country celebrate the life and work of this great man.

THE KING CENTER: Coretta Scott King also worked for nearly 30 years to build the King Center. It is a 23-acre national historic park in Atlanta, Georgia. It includes Dr. King's tomb, a library, museum, and exhibits devoted to education and history. It is also a center for study and learning about Dr. King's life and the movement for Civil Rights.

MARTIN LUTHER KING'S HOME AND FAMILY: Coretta Scott and Martin Luther King Jr. married on June 18, 1953. They had four children, Yolanda, Martin Luther III, Dexter, and Bernice.

HIS LEGACY: Martin Luther King Jr. is considered one of the most important Americans in history. He worked tirelessly to achieve Civil Rights for African-Americans, and dignity for all people. His words and actions inspired Americans of all backgrounds to examine the true meaning of freedom and equality. He was a man of courage and conviction, passionate in his pursuit of the greater good. Through nonviolent demonstrations, he showed how social change could be achieved, without force or bloodshed. He is revered around the world as a man of peace who pursued justice for all.

WORLD WIDE WEB SITES:

http://memory.loc.gov/ammem/today/jan15.html
http://nobelprize.org/cgi-bin/nobel_prizes/peace/laureates/
http://www/kingcenter.org/csk/bio.html
http://www.lib.lsu.edu/hum/mlk/srs216.html
http://www.stanford.edu/group/King/about_king/biography

Malcolm X
1925 - 1965
African-American Political and
Religious Leader and Activist

MALCOLM X WAS BORN on May 19, 1925, in Omaha, Nebraska. "Malcolm X" became his name when he joined the Nation of Islam. When he was born, his name was Malcolm Little. His parents were Louise and Earl Little. Louise was a homemaker and Earl was a Baptist minister. Malcolm was one of eight children. His siblings were named Wilfred, Hilda, Philbert, Reginald, Wesley, Yvonne, and Robert.

MALCOLM X GREW UP in several places. His father, Earl Little, was a follower of **MARCUS GARVEY**. Garvey was a Black Nationalist and separatist. That is, he supported the belief that blacks should live separately from whites. He encouraged blacks to be proud of their African heritage. He urged them to become economically and socially independent of whites. He also declared that American blacks should return to Africa.

Following Garvey's beliefs brought danger to Earl Little and his family. When Malcolm's mother was pregnant with him, the white racist Ku Klux Klan stormed the home. They threatened the family. Soon, the Littles left Omaha.

In 1929, they settled in Lansing, Michigan. Once again, a white racist group threatened them. Their home was burned to the ground. Malcolm recalled that "nightmare night in 1929, my earliest memory. I remember being suddenly snatched awake into a frightening confusion of pistol shots and shouting and smoke and flames."

Later, Earl Little was found murdered. The police claimed that his death and the destruction of their home were accidents. But the Little family knew the racist group had committed the crimes.

Louise Little suffered a breakdown. She was put in a mental hospital and her children were placed in different foster homes. Over the next few years, Malcolm lived in several foster homes in Michigan.

MALCOLM X WENT TO SCHOOL at the public schools. He was an excellent student. In junior high, he was at the top of his class. He loved learning, and he wanted to be a lawyer. But his teachers belittled his ambitions. They told him that blacks couldn't achieve those kinds of goals.

*Malcolm X holds up a newspaper at a Black Muslim rally
in New York City, August 6, 1963.*

Soon, Malcolm lost interest in school. He dropped out. He moved to Boston, where he lived with one of his sisters. He worked at odd jobs around town.

Next, Malcolm moved to the Harlem section of New York City. He got involved with using and selling drugs, and gambling. Moving back to Boston, Malcolm continued to use drugs and began to steal. In 1946, he was arrested for robbery. He was tried and sentenced to prison for 10 years.

PRISON: Malcolm Little entered prison an angry, addicted young man. Just 21 years old, he got into even more trouble in prison. He spent time in solitary confinement. Finally, he met another inmate who introduced him to the library. Malcolm had always loved to read. Now he devoted himself to reading. He recalled "reading everything I could get my hands on." He even copied out the dictionary by hand. He showed his quick mind and intellect in debates with other prisoners.

Malcolm also began to study the Black Muslim faith. His brothers had become members of the Nation of Islam, the official name of the faith. The church was headed by a man named Elijah Muhammad. He claimed that he was the messenger of God, or "Allah," in the Muslim faith.

Elijah Muhammad preached that blacks were superior to whites. The white race was evil, in the eyes of the Black Muslims. White society kept black people from economic and political equality. The Black Muslims wanted a separate nation, for them alone. They also had strict rules about daily life. The rules emphasized cleanliness and forbade smoking, drinking alcohol, and eating pork.

CONVERSION TO THE NATION OF ISLAM: While in prison, Malcolm began to write to Elijah Muhammad. He became a devout Black Muslim. He renamed himself "Malcolm X." His new last name was a symbol of his freedom, for he considered "Little" a slave name. When he left prison in 1952, he moved to Chicago, the home of the Nation of Islam. He began to work closely with Elijah Muhammad.

A FIERY SPOKESMAN FOR THE NATION OF ISLAM: Malcolm X became recognized as a powerful speaker for the Black Muslim faith. He became an assistant minister and opened Muslim Temples in Detroit, Boston, Philadelphia, and New York.

This fiery preacher drew crowds of black people who were captivated by his speeches. He told them that whites had made them feel inferior. "Who taught you to hate the color of your skin? Who taught you to hate the texture of your hair? Who taught you to hate the shape of your nose and lips? You know." He encouraged them to embrace their blackness, and take pride in their heritage.

Malcolm X became the popular face and voice of the Nation of Islam. He spoke all over the country, and drew new members to the faith. He also faced police and federal harassment. Police officers broke into his home in 1958. Soon, his actions were followed by the F.B.I.

Malcolm X continued to act as an important black leader in America. He organized marches against government and police actions he considered racist and unfair. He drew the attention of the media to the continuing racial inequities around the country.

Malcolm was also feared as a radical by many whites. In 1959 he was featured on a TV special called "The Hate That Hate Produced," hosted by Mike Wallace. The program focused on the beliefs of the Nation of Islam. It was the first time many white people had ever heard of the group. Some people found it shocking, but it also spread the word of the faith. And it made Malcolm X a well-known spokesman for Black Muslims.

Malcolm X was controversial among some blacks, too. He openly challenged Civil Rights leaders like **Martin Luther King Jr.**

Malcolm believed that racial equality and integration were foolish goals. He thought that blacks must work for a separate nation or return to Africa. He said they must fight for their rights "by any means necessary."

King believed in civil disobedience and rejected violence. He and Malcolm were at first at odds with one another. But gradually, Malcolm X changed his thinking about race.

BREAKING WITH ELIJAH MUHAMMAD: Malcolm X began to have doubts about the leader of the Nation of Islam, Elijah Muhammad. He felt that the leader and some of his associates were jealous of his popularity. Also, he learned that Elijah Muhammad had been having affairs with female members of the faith. That was against the teachings of the Nation of Islam. Malcolm felt betrayed by those actions.

In March 1964, Malcolm broke with the Nation of Islam. He founded his own religious group, which he called the Muslim Mosque. Soon afterward, he went on a religious pilgrimage.

MECCA: In Islam, the faithful are encouraged to make *hajj*, or a pilgrimage, to Mecca. Mecca is in Saudi Arabia. It is the holiest city in Islam. The journey changed Malcolm's thinking about faith and race. He encountered people from all over the world. He met with Arab leaders and Islamic scholars. He was drawn to their beliefs, which interpreted Islam as a religion for all, not one created along racial lines. He recalled meeting "blonde-haired, blue-eyed men I could call my brothers."

CHANGING BELIEFS: Malcolm X returned to the U.S. a changed man. He was ready to join other African-American leaders in their

Malcolm X and Martin Luther King, Jr.
waiting for a press conference, March 26, 1964.

fight for Civil Rights. He wanted to work with black people of all backgrounds to insure the rights of all. "It's time for us to submerge our differences and realize that it is best for us to first see that we have the same problem," he said. He started his own group, The Organization of Afro-American Unity, to promote his new beliefs.

But his message of harmony upset the leaders of the Nation of Islam. He began to receive death threats. He said he knew he was a "marked man." His house was firebombed, and the death threats continued.

ASSASSINATION: On February 21, 1965, while speaking to a group in New York City, Malcolm X was assassinated. The three men charged with the crime were all members of the Nation of Islam. He was 39 years old.

MALCOLM X'S HOME AND FAMILY: Malcolm X met Betty Shabazz in New York, when he was a minister and she was a teacher at a Nation of Islam temple. They married in 1958. They had six daughters, Attallah, Qubilah, Ilyasah, Gamilah, Malaak, and Malikah. Betty Shabazz continued to work for the causes she and her husband championed until her own death, in 1997.

HIS LEGACY: Though his life ended in 1965, the words of Malcolm X still inspire people today. The same year he was assassinated, his *Autobiography* was published, bringing his beliefs to a wide range of readers. In 1992, Spike Lee made an award-winning film, *Malcolm X*, that introduced another generation to his teachings.

Malcolm X challenged Americans, black and white, to rethink the problems of race. He wasn't afraid to be feared or to be controversial; his voice demanded to be heard. His own thinking on the possibilities of racial equality evolved over his lifetime. He moved from believing in radical separatism to a broader vision of the fight for equality. He is considered one of the most important leaders of the movement for African-American rights in the 20th century.

WORLD WIDE WEB SITES:

http://www.brothermalcolm.net/
http://www.cmgworldwide.com/historic/malcolm/
http://www.columbia.edu/cu/ccbh/mxp/
http://malcolm-x.org/docs/
http://www.pbs.org/wgbh/amex/malcolmx/

Thurgood Marshall
1908 - 1993
African-American Lawyer and Supreme Court Justice
First African-American to Serve
on the U.S. Supreme Court

THURGOOD MARSHALL WAS BORN on July 2, 1908, in Baltimore, Maryland. His parents were William and Norma Marshall. William was a waiter in an all-white club and Norma was a teacher. Thurgood had one brother, Aubrey.

Marshall was the great-grandson of a slave. His first name, Thurgood, was taken from that of his great-grandfather, Thoroughgood. He had been brought to the U.S. from the Congo in the 1800s and forced into slavery.

THURGOOD MARSHALL GREW UP in a comfortable, loving home. His parents encouraged him and his brother to work hard in school, and to ask questions. Marshall remembered his father helping him to learn to reason. "He never told me to become a lawyer, but he turned me into one. He did it by teaching me to argue, by challenging my logic on every point, and by making me prove every statement I made."

Thurgood grew up in a neighborhood where he played with black and white children. Marshall remembered that he was a "cutup" as a child. When he misbehaved, his punishment was to read the U.S. Constitution. He had the document memorized by the age of 18.

THURGOOD MARSHALL WENT TO SCHOOL at the segregated schools of Baltimore. He recalled that he was a "mediocre" student at Frederick Douglass High School. But he did well enough to go to college at Lincoln University in Pennsylvania. It was a traditional black college, and only for males. Among his classmates was Langston Hughes, the famous poet of the Harlem Renaissance. Another classmate was Cab Calloway, who became a famous jazz singer.

Marshall graduated from Lincoln in 1930 and wanted to go to law school. He applied to the University of Maryland. He was denied admission because he was black. It was a moment of great importance for Marshall. In many ways, it set the course for his life. Marshall chose to attend law school at Howard University.

At Howard, Marshall studied law under Charles Hamilton Houston. Houston was a tremendous influence on Marshall. He believed that lawyers should use their skills to promote social justice. He inspired Marshall and his fellow students to believe in the power of the law to change things for good. Houston especially focused on the 1898 Supreme Court decision **PLESSY V. FERGUSON**. That decision brought about the "separate but equal" doctrine that legalized segregation in the U.S.

When Marshall graduated from Howard in 1933, he was first in his class. He was about to begin a law career that would make him one of the most important figures of the **CIVIL RIGHTS MOVEMENT**.

BECOMING A LAWYER: After law school, Marshall started a private law practice. In one of his first cases he defended a black student named Donald Gaines Murray. Murray was a graduate of Amherst College, one of the finest schools in the country. Like Marshall, he had also applied to the University of Maryland's law school. And like Marshall, he had been denied admission, because he was black.

Marshall sued the University of Maryland on Murray's behalf. He claimed that the University's admission policies were unconstitutional. And he won. It was his first major case, and a vindication for Murray, and for all African-Americans.

NAACP: Marshall decided to join the legal team of the **NATIONAL ASSOCIATION FOR THE ADVANCEMENT OF COLORED PEOPLE (NAACP).** His former law professor, Houston, was head of the legal division. When Houston retired, in 1938, Marshall became head of the NAACP's Legal Defense and Education Fund.

Over the next 20 years, Marshall argued and won landmark cases that changed the way African-Americans were treated under

Marshall with client Donald Murray, who was denied entry into the University of Maryland Law School, 1935.

the law. He believed passionately that equal rights for all Americans were guaranteed by the U.S. Constitution. And he believed that those rights could be achieved through the legal system. The cases he took revealed how segregation was unconstitutional. Over the years, the cases he brought before the courts involved discrimination in many areas, especially voting, housing, and education.

THE COURT SYSTEM: The U.S. Court system is divided into several levels. Someone who brings a case to court is called a "plaintiff." If plaintiffs take a case to one level of the courts, and the decision goes against them, they can take the case to an "appeal" court. That system of challenges can continue through all the levels of the system to the U.S. Supreme Court. That is the highest court in the land.

The Supreme Court's decisions always involve the constitutionality of a case. In Marshall's lawsuits, the cases involved the constitutionality of the "separate but equal" concept that had been decided in Plessy v. Ferguson.

ARGUING CASES BEFORE THE SUPREME COURT: As the head lawyer for the NAACP, Marshall devoted himself to ending discrimination through the legal system. He knew the reality of what "separate but equal" meant to African-Americans. He knew that facilities and opportunities for blacks—schools, houses, jobs, transportation—were separate, but *never* equal.

Marshall's cases often took him to the South, where racism was a way of life. On many occasions, his life was threatened. But he refused to let that stop him.

In 1944, he argued an important case involving voting rights. He convinced the Court that excluding blacks from voting in primaries was unconstitutional. In 1948, he successfully argued against racial discrimination in buying houses. In 1950, he won two cases involving inequality in education.

But it was another education case that made him, and the name of the case, part of U.S. history.

BROWN V. THE BOARD OF EDUCATION: In 1954, Marshall was one of the NAACP attorneys arguing a case called "Brown v. the Board of Education of Topeka." (Legal cases are named for the two sides in the suit. In this case, Marshall and the NAACP represented Oliver Brown against the Topeka, Kansas, Board of Education.)

Marshall and Roy Wilkins at work in an NAACP office, 1943.

At that time, 17 states and the District of Columbia had laws that segregated schools. In some states the decision was left up to individual school districts. In Topeka, Kansas, schools were legally segregated. All over the country, black children went to schools where buildings were crumbling and books were scarce. The states could *legally* spend more on white students, their teachers, and their facilities than on black students.

Oliver Brown, an African-American, was the father of seven-year-old Linda Brown. He filed the suit on Linda's behalf. Linda had to travel 1 hour 20 minutes to get to her segregated school each day. The school was 21 blocks from her home. She had to cross a dangerous railroad yard every day to get to the bus that took her to school.

Linda's white neighbors walked to a whites-only school that was just 7 blocks from her home. The NAACP claimed that such treatment was unconstitutional.

The new Chief Justice of the Supreme Court was named Earl Warren. He listened to Marshall argue the Brown case. He wrote the Court's response. He agreed with Marshall's argument. He called education "perhaps the most important function of state and local government." He also wrote:

"Does segregation of children in the public schools solely on the basis of race deprive the children of the minority group of equal educational opportunity? We believe it does.

"In the field of education, the doctrine of 'separate but equal' has no place. Separated education facilities are inherently unequal."

With that decision, the Supreme Court declared segregation unconstitutional. It took many years to integrate the public schools, but the Brown decision marked the end of legal discrimination based on race. It was one of the most important decisions of the century. It led to the end of segregation in all public facilities.

Marshall was called on again to fight segregation in the schools. After the success of **BROWN V. THE BOARD OF EDUCATION**, the **NAACP** brought court cases against school districts that were slow to comply with court-ordered desegregation of their public schools. One of those districts was Little Rock. **DAISY BATES,** head of the Arkansas NAACP, organized a group of nine students to integrate Little Rock's Central High School.

The nine students were Minnijean Brown, Elizabeth Eckford, Ernest Green, Thelma Mothershed, Melba Patillo, Gloria Ray, Terrence Roberts, Jefferson Thomas, and Carolotta Walls. Together, they faced an angry mob of citizens when they first tried to attend Central in September 1957. Over the course of several days, the mob became violent, and the students and their supporters were heckled, taunted, and some of them were attacked. TV newscasters broadcast the scene of racial chaos and hatred around the world. President Dwight D. Eisenhower became involved, sending U.S. paratroopers in to protect the students and enforce the desegregation agreement.

"MR. CIVIL RIGHTS": Marshall became a famous man. He became known as "Mr. Civil Rights." He continued to argue cases before the Court. His actions led to the **VOTING RIGHTS ACT** and the **CIVIL RIGHTS ACT**. This champion of equality argued a total of 32 cases before the Supreme Court. He won 29.

Marshall found time to help out the cause of Civil Rights in other countries, too. England and the United Nations asked him to help write the constitutions for the new African countries of Ghana and Tanzania.

U.S. COURT OF APPEALS: In 1961, President John F. Kennedy appointed Marshall to the U.S. Court of Appeals. That Court hears appeals from lower court decisions. The judges on the Appeals Court listen to cases, then write their opinions. In four years, Marshall wrote over 150 decisions for the Court of Appeals. The subjects of the cases often concerned individual rights, including privacy and immigrant rights.

SOLICITOR GENERAL: In 1965, President Lyndon Johnson appointed Marshall Solicitor General. The Solicitor General argues

Marshall (center) with George Hayes and
James Nabrit celebrating their Supreme Court victory
in the Brown v. the Board of Education case, 1954.

the U.S. Government's side of legal cases before the Supreme Court. In two years as Solicitor General, Marshall argued 19 cases, and won 14.

SUPREME COURT JUSTICE: In 1967, President Johnson named Marshall to the U.S. Supreme Court. He was the first African-American ever to serve on the Court. And, he was certainly one of the high court's most qualified candidates. In his distinguished career, he represented, and won, more cases before the Supreme Court than any other lawyer in history.

Marshall served on the Supreme Court from 1967 until 1991. In those years, he continued to promote anti-discrimination in the cases before the Court. He defended equal access to education, jobs, and housing. He also believed that people needed to have access to legal aid, even if they were poor. Marshall championed these values in his decisions and opinions throughout his 24 years on the Court. He retired from the Supreme Court in 1991, for health reasons.

THURGOOD MARSHALL'S HOME AND FAMILY: Marshall was married twice. While in college, he met and fell in love with Vivian Burey, whose nickname was Buster. They married in 1929. Buster died of cancer in 1955. His second wife was named Cecilia Suyat. They married in 1955 and had two sons, Thurgood Jr. and John.

Marshall's health began to fail in the early 1990s. He retired from the Court in 1991 and died of heart failure on January 24, 1993.

LEGACY: Thurgood Marshall was one of the most important figures of the Civil Rights Movement. As a lawyer and a judge, he believed that the Constitution guaranteed legal rights for all. He argued cases not just for African-Americans, but for all people seeking equality in the justice system.

WORLD WIDE WEB SITES:

http://chnm.gmu/edu/courses/122/hill/marshall.htm
http://memory.loc.gov/ammem/today/oct02.html
http://www.landmarkcases.org/brown/marshall.html
http://www.oyez.org/justices/thurgood_marshall
http://www.thurgoodmarshall.com/interviews/

Elijah McCoy
1844(?) - 1929
Canadian-Born American Inventor
Inventor of the Automatic Lubricating Cup
"The Real McCoy"

ELIJAH McCOY WAS BORN in Colchester, Ontario, Canada. The exact year of his birth isn't known for sure, but is thought to be either 1843 or 1844. His father, George, and his mother, Mildred, were fugitives slaves from Kentucky. They had escaped to Canada using the Underground Railroad.

In 1837, war broke out between the French-speaking people of Upper Canada and the English-speaking people of Lower Canada. George McCoy enlisted in the army and served with the English-speaking forces. When the war ended, he was given 160 acres of farmland near Colchester for his service. That's where Elijah was born.

ELIJAH McCOY GREW UP and went to the local public school for black children in Colchester. As a boy, he showed great interest in the machines and tools that were used on the family farm. He loved to take things apart and put them back together. His parents recognized his mechanical talents. They saved enough money to send him to school in Edinburgh, Scotland.

ELIJAH THE ENGINEER: At the age of 15 Elijah went to Scotland to learn about mechanical engineering. He spent five years studying in Edinburgh. He returned to Canada as a master mechanic and engineer.

When the American Civil War ended in 1865, the McCoy family moved back to the U.S. They settled in Ypsilanti, Michigan. Elijah tried to find work as an engineer, but because he was black there were not many jobs available to him.

He finally got a position as a fireman and oiler on the Michigan Central Railroad in 1870. This was a good job because many times the firemen were promoted to locomotive driver.

Physically, it was hard work. As the fireman, McCoy had to shovel two tons of coal into the firebox of a locomotive engine every hour. And as the oiler, he had to grease the moving parts of the locomotives every few miles. That meant that the trains had to stop frequently, just to be oiled.

McCoy's quick mind and engineering background led him to think of a better way to oil the moving parts of the locomotives. If there were some way to automatically drip oil onto these screws, axles, and bearings when it was needed, the trains would not have to stop every few miles for lubrication by hand.

THE AUTOMATIC LUBRICATING CUP: For two years McCoy experimented with a design in a home-made machine shop in Ypsilanti. When he was finished, he had created a special cup that held oil. The cup used steam pressure to push a piston and allowed oil to be released into tubes that carried the oil to the engine's operating parts.

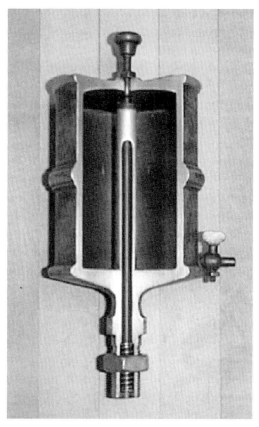

Replica of McCoy's 1872 lubricator.

On June 23, 1872, McCoy was issued a patent for his invention. He took his lubricating cup to the engineers of the Michigan Central Railroad. Soon the cups were installed on locomotive engines. Now the engines didn't have to stop every few miles to be oiled by hand. Not only was the lubrication process easier, but the lubricating cups made the engines last longer and need fewer repairs.

McCoy's cup also allowed machines to remain in motion while they were oiled. This completely changed the railroad industry. It could also be used in factory machinery.

There were some who thought that a black man could not make a worthy invention. They tried to discourage others from buying McCoy's cup. But the engineers at Michigan Central Railroad gave him a chance. They hired McCoy to teach the engineers and technicians how to use the oil cups. Before long McCoy's cups were being installed on locomotives, steamships, and heavy machinery.

Between 1872 and 1876 McCoy was granted six patents for lubricators and one for a folding ironing board.

THE REAL McCOY: As McCoy's lubricating cup became popular, others tried to copy his design. None of them were able to produce an oil cup that was as reliable as McCoy's. It is said that buyers began to ask, "Is this the real McCoy?" The expression continues to be used today when people want to make sure they are getting the genuine item.

McCOY IN DETROIT: In 1882 McCoy moved to Detroit, Michigan. He continued to work on inventions and also offered expertise and advice to the Detroit Lubricator Company and other firms. Between 1886 and 1926 McCoy was granted more than 45 patents. All but eight were for lubricating devices.

As the railroads began to carry more materials and passengers across the land it became clear that they needed larger locomotives. To power these engines a superheated steam process began to be used. While superheating allowed the engines to go more miles on less coal, it also caused new problems in lubrication.

In April 1915, McCoy was granted a patent for what he called his best invention, the "Locomotive Lubricator." This was a lubricator that used oil mixed with powdered graphite. McCoy's lubricator was effective and efficient and helped keep the superheated engines running smoothly while using less fuel.

THE McCOY MANUFACTURING COMPANY: To make and sell his locomotive lubricator, McCoy established his own business in 1920. By 1923 he had become well known in the manufacturing industry. He was still active at 80. He spent time working with young people in Detroit, encouraging them to work hard so that they, too, could have productive lives.

LAST YEARS: In 1923 Elijah and his wife, Mary, were involved in a car accident. Mary never fully recovered from her injuries and died shortly afterward. After her death, Elijah's health began to fail as well. He died on October 10, 1929.

ELIJAH McCOY'S HOME AND FAMILY: In 1868 Elijah married Ann Elizabeth Stuart. She passed away four years later. In 1873 he married Mary Eleanora Delaney Brownlow. She became his partner for the next 50 years. They had one child.

HIS LEGACY: Elijah McCoy never became rich from his inventions. He sold some of his important patents, but never received much money from the companies who profited from his creations.

McCoy contributed to the success of steam engines during the years when they were the main source of transportation. His contribution to the lubrication of machinery changed the way factories were run. Besides his famous lubricators, McCoy invented the first folding ironing board and also a lawn sprinkler. He is credited with inventing a buggy top support, a tread for tires, scaffold support, a rubber heel and a steam dome for locomotives.

Versions of McCoy's original lubricating cup are still in use today in factories, mining machinery, construction equipment, naval boats, and space craft.

WORLD WIDE WEB SITES:

http://www.africawithin.com/bios/elijah_mccoy.htm
http://www.blackhistorysociety.ca/EmcCoy.htm
http://www.blackinventor.com/pages/elijahmccoy.html

Garrett Morgan
1877 - 1963
African-American Inventor of the
Traffic Signal and the Gas Mask

GARRETT MORGAN WAS BORN on March 4, 1877, in Paris, Kentucky. His full name was Garrett Augustus Morgan. His parents were Sydney and Elizabeth Morgan. Sydney was a farmer and Elizabeth was a homemaker. Garrett was the seventh of 11 children.

GARRETT MORGAN GREW UP in the small town of Paris. His family was very poor. Both of his parents had been slaves. They were freed in 1863 during the **CIVIL WAR**, which lasted from 1861 to 1865. Yet even after the Civil War, when all blacks were free, they faced discrimination. It was hard for African-Americans to get a good education, a good job, or good housing. Many black families, like Morgan's, were poor.

GARRETT MORGAN WENT TO SCHOOL at an all-black school in Kentucky. He only finished the fifth grade. At the age of 14, he decided to leave home and move north. He hoped to find more opportunity and build a new life.

MOVING NORTH: With very little money, but with ambition and hope, Morgan moved to Cincinnati, Ohio, in 1891. There, he found work as a handyman for a wealthy white landowner.

After four years in Cincinnati, Morgan moved to Cleveland, Ohio. He wanted to find better work for better pay. In Cleveland, he found a job repairing sewing machines.

BECOMING AN INVENTOR: Morgan discovered that he had a knack for fixing things. He liked to take machines apart and figure out how they could work better. In doing that, he made his first invention. It was a part for a sewing machine, and it made him $50.

In 1907, Morgan opened his own sewing machine shop. The store was very successful, and he made good money. He was able to buy a house and get married.

Morgan next opened a tailor shop, where he and his workers made clothes. While working in the tailor shop one night, he created another product. He accidently used a cloth made of curly pony fur to wipe polish off his hands. Several hours later, he noticed that the fur was straight.

Morgan was excited by his newest discovery. He knew that the polish could be used as a hair straightener. He used it on his neighbor's wiry-haired terrier, and it straightened the dog's hair. Morgan next tried it on his own hair, and it straightened that, too. Soon Morgan had another moneymaking business on his hands, as many curly-haired people bought his product to straighten their hair.

THE GAS MASK: Morgan's next invention was the gas mask. At that time, there was nothing that could protect firefighters or others who work with harmful smoke or gasses. The "Morgan helmet" was a helmet connected to a long hose. The end of the hose was lined with material that could absorb harmful gases.

In 1912, Morgan applied for a patent for his breathing device. His gas mask was a terrific success. He sold it through a new company he created called the National Safety Device Company. Morgan also brought in white partners to help sell the device. Sadly, racism was still a major force in America. Some people would not buy a product created by a black person.

A HERO: On July 24, 1916, Garrett Morgan became a hero. There was a huge explosion in a tunnel below Lake Erie that trapped several workers. The gasses released during the explosion could kill the trapped men.

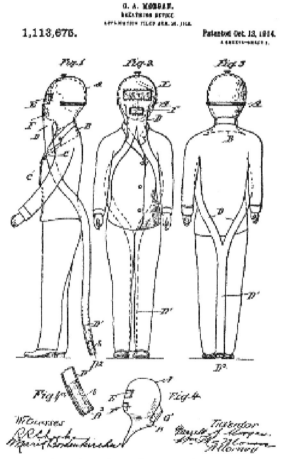

Morgan's first safety helmet. (*Courtesy of Garrett A. Morgan, Jr.*)

Patent drawing for Morgan's gas mask, 1914.

Morgan, his brother Frank, and two other rescue workers put on Morgan's gas masks and rescued the trapped workers. All of Cleveland honored Morgan as a hero. He was named the city's "most honored and bravest citizen."

Morgan's gas mask also saved the lives of thousands of soldiers during World War I (1914-1918). The German army used poison gasses against American soldiers and their allies. Thanks to Morgan's invention, those soldiers' lives were saved.

THE THREE-LIGHT TRAFFIC SIGNAL: Morgan's next major invention came about in the 1920s. By that time, there were many automobiles and horse-drawn carriages crowding the streets of America. But there was no organized way of controlling traffic.

What concerned Morgan most was the accidents that occurred at intersections. Where traffic from one street ran into traffic from another street, there was no way of determining who had the right of way.

So Morgan invented the traffic signal. It controlled stop-and-go traffic at intersections. Morgan created a "three-way signal." It had three arms that swung out in turn, with the words "Stop," "Go," and "Caution." Later, after traffic signals became electric, those signals became our modern "Red," "Green," and "Yellow" lights.

Morgan's invention made streets safer all over the world. His traffic signal was also used to control train traffic.

Morgan received a patent for his traffic signal in 1923. He sold the patent to the General Electric Company for $40,000. That was a great deal of money at that time.

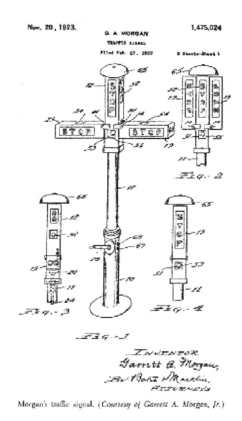

Nov. 20, 1923.   1,475,024
G. A. MORGAN
TRAFFIC SIGNAL
Filed Feb. 27, 1922   2 Sheets-Sheet 1

Morgan's traffic signal. *(Courtesy of Garrett A. Morgan, Jr.)*

Patent drawing for Morgan's traffic signal, 1923.

Morgan also devoted much of his life to improving the treatment of blacks in American society. He started a newspaper, called the *Cleveland Call*, that covered news about African-Americans. He was also active in political organizations that promoted equality for blacks.

After a long and productive life, Morgan died in 1963, at the age of 86.

GARRETT MORGAN'S HOME AND FAMILY: Garrett Morgan married his wife, Mary Anne, in 1908. They had three sons, John, Garrett Jr., and Cosmo.

GARRETT A. MORGAN TECHNOLOGY AND TRANSPORTATION FUTURES PROGRAM: The U.S. Department of Transportation has a program named after Garrett Morgan. The purpose of the program is to get young people interested in the field of transportation. It encourages them to study transportation and take jobs in the field.

HIS LEGACY: Through his invention of the traffic signal, Morgan made a major contribution to public safety. His name lives on in a program devoted to helping others through education and job opportunities. His invention of the gas mask also saved thousands of lives in World War I. He was inducted into the Inventors Hall of Fame in 2005.

WORLD WIDE WEB SITES:

http://education.dot.gov/aboutmorgan.html

http://web.mit.edu/invent/iow/morgan.html

http://www.invent.org/hall_of_fame/224.html

http://www.sciencemuseum.org/uk/on-line/garret-morgan/

http://www.uh.edu/engines/epi1624.htm

Jesse Owens
1913 - 1980
African-American Track Athlete
and Olympic Gold Medalist

JESSE OWENS WAS BORN on September 12, 1913, in Oakville, Alabama. His full name was James Cleveland Owens. His parents were Henry and Mary Owens. He had six older brothers and three older sisters.

JESSE OWENS GREW UP on the family farm. His parents were sharecroppers. Sharecroppers did not own the land they worked on. They paid rent to a land owner in the form of a portion of their crops. What was left was theirs to sell or eat. Many African-Americans and poor whites in the American South lived and worked this way. Their life was very poor and bleak, especially if the weather was bad and the harvest was small.

When Jesse was nine, the family moved to Cleveland, Ohio. His parents hoped for better wages and more opportunities for their family. His father and brothers found work in steel mills. Jesse helped out, too, working several part-time jobs.

JESSE OWENS WENT TO SCHOOL at the public schools in Cleveland. He attended Bolton Elementary. Even though he was nine, he was put into the first grade. When he proved he could read, he moved up to second grade.

At that time, Jesse was known in his family by his initials, "J.C." In school the teacher mispronounced his nickname as "Jesse." The name stuck.

At Fairmount Junior High, Jesse drew the attention of teacher and coach Charles Riley. Riley could tell Jesse had talent. He offered to train him in track and field events. Because Jesse had to work after school, Riley coached him every morning.

Jesse responded to the training like the champion he was. He started winning races and breaking world records for his age group. He was a sprinter, running the 100-yard and 220-yard dash. He was also an excellent jumper, in both the high jump and the long jump.

Jesse went on to East Technical High in Cleveland. Riley continued to coach the young sensation. In June 1933 at the national high

Owens wins the 220-yard dash at the Big Ten Conference Track and Field
meet held in Ann Arbor, Mich., May 25, 1935.
Owens broke three world records that day.

school championships, he became a national star. Owens won the long jump, set the record for the 220-yard dash, and tied the world record for the 100-yard dash.

COLLEGE—THE OHIO STATE UNIVERSITY: In 1933, Owens began college at Ohio State University. Already a great athlete, at a track meet in Ann Arbor, Michigan, in 1935, he became a legend. At the Big Ten championship on May 25, 1935, Owens broke the world records in the 220-yard dash and 220-yard hurdles. He also broke the world record distance in the long jump. In the winning jump, Owens set a record of 26 feet, 8 inches, a record that stood for 25 years. To top that off, he tied the world record time for the 100-

yard dash. His performance that day is considered one of the finest by a college athlete, ever.

RACIAL AND ACADEMIC PROBLEMS: As one of only a few black students at Ohio State, Owens faced racial prejudice. On campus and at track meets, he had to put up with racial slurs. He had to live off campus, with other black athletes. When the team traveled, Owens and the other African-Americans often couldn't sleep or eat with their white teammates.

Owens struggled in his classes, and was put on academic probation. He was ineligible for the indoor track season in the winter of 1936 because of poor grades. Yet despite those challenges, Jesse Owens became an international star, and symbol of greatness and dignity, in 1936.

OLYMPIC TRIUMPHS: In 1936, Owens was part of an Olympic team that made history. That year, the Olympic Games were in Berlin, Germany. It was only three years before the outbreak of World War II. There was great tension in Europe and the world because of the rise of Nazism in Germany under Adolf Hitler. Hitler and the Nazi Party believed that the white race was superior, and that Germans were the pinnacle of human perfection.

At the 1936 Olympics, in a stadium that included Hitler in the crowd, Jesse Owens quietly but decisively defied the racist propaganda of the Nazis. Winning four gold medals, he entered the record books, and the hearts and minds of people around the world.

Owens won his first gold medal in the 100-meter dash in 10.3 seconds, edging out Ralph Metcalfe, also an African-American. His next medal came in the long jump. His major competitor was Luz Long, a tall, blue-eyed, blond German. Owens won the gold medal with a final jump of 26 feet, 5¼ inches. Long congratulated the African-American champion.

"It took a lot of courage for him to befriend me in front of Hitler," Owens recalled. "You can melt down all the medals and cups I have and they wouldn't be a plating on the 24-karat friend-ship I felt for Luz Long at that moment. Hitler must have gone crazy watching us embrace."

Next, Owens medaled in the 200-meter dash. Once again, he set an Olympic record of 20.7 seconds. His final gold medal came as part of the 4x100 relay team. With Owens running leadoff, the U.S. team won by 15 yards. Their world-record time would last 20 years.

In the face of racial hatred, Owens had triumphed. He was the first American ever to win four gold medals. And he'd set two world records and two Olympic records in the process.

BACK TO AMERICA: Owens returned to a hero's welcome and a parade. But the U.S. was still mired in the same kind of racial dis-crimination he'd known before. "When I came back to my native country, after all the stories about Hitler, I couldn't ride in the front of the bus," he said. "I had to go to the back door. I couldn't live where I wanted. I wasn't invited to shake hands with Hitler, but I wasn't invited to the White House to shake hands with the Presi-dent, either."

FIRST JOBS: Owens decided to leave school. He became a public speaker and did other jobs to provide for his family. He also com-

Owens (center) at the medal ceremony for the long jump
at the 1936 Olympics in Berlin, Germany.
He was the first athlete ever to win four gold medals in a single Olympics.

peted in several outlandish running competitions, against horses, or against baseball players. "People said it was degrading for an Olympic champion to run against a horse, but what was I supposed to do?" Owens said. "I had four gold medals, but you can't eat four gold medals."

Owens winning the broad jump at the National AAU Championships,
in Princeton, N.J., 1936.

He ran a dry cleaning business for a while, but it failed. Owens had to declare bankruptcy. He got a job with the Ford Motor company during World War II.

Owens moved to Chicago after the war. He served as a public speaker to youth groups and other organizations. He was director of Chicago's South Side Boys' Club, and held positions on the Illinois Youth Commission and the Illinois State Athletic Commission.

GOODWILL AMBASSADOR: In 1955 the U.S. State Department asked Owens to travel to India, Malaysia, and the Philippines. There he spoke about the American way of life and ran athletic clinics. In 1956 he attended the Melbourne Olympic Games in Australia as the official U.S. goodwill representative. He was one of the first appointed by President Dwight Eisenhower to the People to People program, which promoted world peace and understanding.

In 1964, Owens started the Jesse Owens Games. The competition was sponsored by the Atlantic Richfield Company. Over a million boys and girls competed in the games each year.

Many honors came to Owens late in life. In 1972 Ohio State awarded him an honorary doctorate of athletic arts. In 1974 he was inducted into the Track and Field Hall of Fame. In 1976 President Gerald Ford presented Owens the Medal of Freedom. Finally, President Jimmy Carter honored him in 1979 with the Living Legends Award for encouraging others to "reach for greatness."

JESSE OWENS'S HOME AND FAMILY: Owens married his high school sweetheart, Minnie Ruth Solomon, in 1935. They had three daughters, Gloria, Marlene, and Beverly.

Owens was a lifelong cigarette smoker. In December 1979 he was diagnosed with lung cancer. Four months later, on March 31, 1980, he died. He was buried in Chicago.

HIS LEGACY: Jesse Owens will forever be remembered for the courage and greatness he showed at the 1936 Olympics. He overcame poverty and racism to become one of the finest athletes and distinguished symbols of African-American achievement in the nation's history.

WORLD WIDE WEB SITES:

http://www.jesseowens.org
http://library.osu.edu/sites/archives/owens
http://www.mccsc.edu/~jcmslib/mlk/owwens/biography.htm

Satchel Paige
1906 - 1982
African-American Professional Baseball Player
Star of Negro League Baseball and
Pioneer in Major League Baseball

SATCHEL PAIGE WAS BORN on July 7, 1906, in Mobile, Alabama.
"Satchel" is a nickname. His full name was Leroy Robert Paige. His
parents were John and Lula Paige. John was a gardener and Lula
was a domestic worker. Satchel had eleven brothers and sisters.
The family lived in a poor area of the city, in a four-room home
near Mobile Bay.

SATCHEL PAIGE GREW UP in Mobile. He started to earn money for his family by working at the Mobile train station. He would carry bags for passengers. That's how he earned his nickname, "Satchel." He devised a sort of harness that allowed him to carry more satchels, or traveling bags, than anyone else at the station.

SATCHEL PAIGE WENT TO SCHOOL at W.H. Council School in Mobile. He began playing baseball for the school team when he was 10 years old. But he was not a model student. He got into trouble for playing hooky and getting into fights.

REFORM SCHOOL AND BASEBALL: At age 12 Satchel was caught stealing toy rings from a store. He was sent to reform school, the Industrial School for Negro Children at Mount Meigs, Alabama. The school was far from his home, near the state capital, Montgomery. Satchel spent five-and-a-half years at the school. He later said, "They made a man out of me . . . and gave me a chance to polish up my baseball game." His coach at the school, Edward Byrd, taught him how to pitch, including his trademark high leg kick.

"JIM CROW" AND THE NEGRO LEAGUES: In the early part of the 20th century racial segregation was widespread in America. Especially in southern states, a practice referred to as **"JIM CROW"** separated public facilities, such as restrooms and drinking fountains, into areas for whites and blacks.

Schools in the South and elsewhere were segregated by race. And in baseball, at nearly all levels, white and black players did not play against each other. Black professional players had their own leagues, the Negro Leagues. It was there that Satchel Paige debuted in 1924, for the Mobile Tigers. He was 6 feet 3 inches tall, and weighed only 140 pounds. Despite his slender stature, he was an immediate success as a pitcher, and a crowd favorite. His pay was one dollar for games that he won.

Unlike teams in the all-white Major Leagues, the Negro League teams didn't offer the players regular pay. The teams traveled from game to game anyway they could. They stayed in cheap hotels, and played in rundown ballparks. Players often changed teams, either because their team went out of business, or just to earn better pay. Some played for more than one team in a season.

EARLY CAREER: In his first several seasons, Paige played for the Mobile Tigers, the Chattanooga Black Lookouts, the Birmingham Black Barons, and the Nashville Elite Giants. The Nashville team moved to Cleveland in 1931. That was during the Depression, a time when up to one-quarter of Americans couldn't find work.

Paige pitching for the
Kansas City Monarchs, 1939.

With the economy suffering and many people unemployed, the team folded before the season ended.

Paige was now a rising star, and had filled out to 180 pounds. As a free agent, he signed on to play for Gus Greenlee, owner of the Pittsburgh Crawfords. Greenlee wanted to assemble the best black players and form the top team in the country. Aside from Paige, Greenlee signed future Baseball Hall of Famers Josh Gibson, Cool Papa Bell, Judy Johnson, and Oscar Charleston. Their home was Greenlee Field, the first black-owned stadium in America. They played in the Negro National League, which Greenlee helped to reestablish.

Paige also played on other teams for extra money. In 1935 he left the Crawfords to play in North Dakota, but returned in 1936. Then he was offered $30,000, a small fortune then, to form a team to play in the Dominican Republic. Paige took the offer, and his team won the island championship. Then, he returned to the U.S. to play exhibitions.

BARNSTORMING: In a type of play known as "barnstorming," Paige's team traveled from town to town, playing against teams of white major leaguers or semipros. They'd take a share of the admission fees for pay. Many teams played this circuit around the country in the 1930s.

Paige was a major box-office draw. He had a variety of different "windmill" windups. His high leg kick was followed by a fastball that was clocked at 103 miles per hour. His control was legendary. One batter said he could throw six out of ten fastballs for strikes over an area the size of a gum wrapper.

Paige warms up in Yankee Stadium for a Negro League game between the Kansas City Monarchs and the New York Cuban Stars, 1942.

AN INJURY AND A SETBACK: While pitching in the Mexican League in 1938, Paige developed a sore pitching arm. It could have ended his career. But he returned to the U.S. and kept at it. While barnstorming for the Kansas City Monarchs, he developed several off-speed pitches. One was his famous "hesitation pitch." He delayed releasing the ball until the last moment, and got batters to swing too early.

STARDOM: In 1940 Paige's pitching arm was healthy again. He had several other pitches to mix in with his fastball. Playing for the

Kansas City Monarchs, he dominated the Negro Leagues in the early and middle 1940s.

When the U.S. entered World War II in 1941, Paige tried to enlist. He was rejected because, at 35, he was considered too old. Still, Paige did what he could for the war effort. He visited military camps and hospitals, to the delight of soldiers.

MAJOR LEAGUE ROOKIE AT 42: In 1948, **Jackie Robinson** became the first black player in baseball's Major Leagues. Paige finally got his chance, too. Owner Bill Veeck of the Cleveland Indians needed a pitcher and signed Paige to a contract at the age of 42. Paige became the first black pitcher in the Majors, and the oldest rookie ever.

During the close of the 1948 season Paige posted a record of 6–1. He was a huge draw for Cleveland. On August 20, 1948, the crowd at the stadium numbered 78,382. That was the largest night-game attendance in baseball history. Paige was the first black player to pitch in the World Series in 1948, which the Indians won. He was named Rookie of the Year.

Veeck sold the Indians in 1949. Paige returned to independent baseball until Veeck bought the St. Louis Browns in 1951. Veeck signed him again, and Paige won 12 games that season. He was selected to be on the American League All-Star team.

CLOSING OUT A LONG CAREER: After two seasons with the Browns, Paige left the majors to play in minor leagues and exhibitions. He returned in 1965, to play for the Kansas City Athletics. The owners wanted to help him qualify for a major-league pension. But they also knew that Paige could draw fans. He sat in a rocking

Paige pitching for the Kansas City Athletics, 1965.

chair in the bullpen. But he still had power. He pitched three shutout innings in 1965. At 59, he was the oldest player ever to appear in a major league game.

In 1967, Paige played for the Indianapolis Clowns, the last of the black baseball teams. In 1968 he coached briefly for the Atlanta Braves, then closed out his major league career.

SATCHEL PAIGE'S HOME AND FAMILY: Paige was married in 1934 to Janet Howard, but the two soon parted ways. In 1947, he married LaHoma Brown. The couple had six children. After he retired, Satchel lived with his family in Kansas City, Missouri.

HALL OF FAME: In 1971 Satchel Paige was inducted into the Baseball Hall of Fame. In his induction speech he said, "Baseball turned me from a second-class citizen to a second-class immortal."

On June 5, 1982, Kansas City honored Satchel Paige by dedicating its youth baseball field to him. Three days later, on June 8, 1982, Paige died at his Kansas City home.

HIS LEGACY: It is estimated that Satchel Paige won more than 2,000 games in his professional career, including 55 no-hitters. He played before as many as 10 million fans. In one season he estimated that he pitched 134 games. Whatever the actual numbers, there is no doubt that Satchel Paige was one of the greatest pitchers of all time. He was a true baseball pioneer, beloved by generations of fans.

WORLD WIDE WEB SITES:

http://www.satchelpaige.com
http://espn.go.com/sportscentury/features/00016396.html
http://www.baseballhalloffame.org/hofers_and_honorees/hofer_bios
   /Paige_Satchel.htm

Rosa Parks
1913 - 2005
African-American Civil Rights Leader

ROSA PARKS WAS BORN on February 4, 1913, in Tuskegee, Alabama. Her name when she was born was Rosa McCauley. Her mother, Leona McCauley, was a teacher. Her father, James McCauley, was a carpenter. She had one brother named Sylvester.

ROSA PARKS GREW UP in Pine Level, Alabama. She moved there with her mother and brother to live on her grandparents farm after her parents divorced. Rosa helped out on the farm, picking vegetables and cotton. The family was poor, but they always had enough to eat.

GROWING UP UNDER JIM CROW: Rosa grew up at a time when black people did not have the same rights as white people. Black people could not buy houses or find jobs where they wanted to. In the South, they couldn't use the same buildings as white people. Blacks had to use different restaurants, movie theaters, even drinking fountains.

Hate groups like the Ku Klux Klan could beat and even murder black people and not be punished. Rosa remembered lying in bed at night and listening to the Klan ride by. Her grandfather would sit up at night by the door with a shotgun to protect them.

ROSA PARKS WENT TO SCHOOL at the black elementary school in her town. Schools were segregated in the South. Black children did not go to school with white children. Black schools were poor and had fewer books and supplies than white schools. Many blacks could not go to high school because there were not high schools for blacks in many areas. That is what happened to Rosa. After she finished junior high, she couldn't go on to high school because there wasn't one in her town for black students.

Around this time, Rosa's grandfather died and her mother and grandmother became ill. Rosa needed to leave school and help out with the family. She finished her high school degree later, through a local college.

ROSA PARKS'S FIRST JOB was sewing clothes for other people. She was living in the city of Montgomery, Alabama, with her husband, Raymond. She and Raymond became active in the fight for

CIVIL RIGHTS for blacks. They joined the **NAACP (NATIONAL AS-SOCIATION FOR THE ADVANCEMENT OF COLORED PEOPLE)** to help in the fight for equality for blacks.

At that time, blacks could not sit in the same section of the bus as whites. A black person had to enter a bus at the front and pay the fare. Then they had to get out of the bus and get back in at the back. Rosa rode the bus to work each day. Each day she had to sit in an area for blacks only.

THE MONTGOMERY BUS BOYCOTT: Rosa Parks became a hero for challenging a law she found racist and intolerable. It happened on a bus in Montgomery, Alabama, on December 1, 1955. On that day, Parks took a seat in the first row of the "blacks only" section of the bus. A white man got on and found that all the seats in the white section were taken. The bus driver told the people in Rosa's row to stand and give their seats to the white man. Park's wouldn't do it.

"I had had enough," she recalls. "I wanted to be treated like a human being." The driver told her she had to move. She wouldn't. He said he would call the police. She told him to go ahead. Rosa Parks was arrested that day for refusing to give her seat on the bus to a white man.

Black Civil Rights leaders asked Parks to challenge the law that allowed her to be arrested. She agreed, even though she knew she would be in danger. Civil Rights groups used her case to plan the Montgomery Bus Boycott. They asked black people not to ride the buses in Montgomery until the laws were changed.

Rosa Parks being fingerprinted after her arrest for refusing to move to the back of a bus in Montgomery, AL, in 1955.

It was a great sacrifice for most of the blacks in Montgomery. Many were poor and needed the bus to get to work. But they stood behind Rosa and the Civil Rights leaders. Almost all the blacks "boycotted," or did not use, the buses.

People all over the country became involved in the Montgomery Bus Boycott. They organized, raised money, and let people all over the country know how unfair the laws were. Some people in the Civil Rights movement were arrested and sent to jail for their work on the boycott. One of them was **Dr. Martin Luther King Jr.**

Rosa Parks riding a bus in Montgomery, AL.

In 1956, the U.S. Supreme Court declared that Alabama's segregated bus system was unconstitutional. It was a great triumph for the Civil Rights movement.

Because of their work on the boycott, Parks and her husband lost their jobs. They received threats from people who hated them for what they did. They decided to move to Detroit, Michigan. For many years Parks worked in the office of a black congressman, John Conyers.

Parks was especially interested in working with young people. She wanted them to know about the fight for Civil Rights. She and Raymond set up the Rosa and Raymond Parks Institute for Self-Development. There young people could take courses in black history and learn about the Civil Rights movement.

ROSA PARKS'S HOME AND FAMILY:
Rosa and Raymond Parks were married in 1932. They lived together in Detroit until his death in 1977. They never had children of their own. They devoted much of their time to the education and care of children through their Institute.

Rosa Parks with South African President Nelson Mandela.

Parks lived in Detroit until her death in 2005. Her casket was placed in the rotunda of the U.S. Capitol for two days. Thousands of people paid their respects to this beloved Civil Rights leader. Her funeral in Detroit was attended by people from all over the country.

HER LEGACY: Parks is remembered for her courage in the face of racism, and for beginning one of the most important protests in the Civil Rights Movement. She was a humble woman who devoted her life to peace and justice. She said, "If I were to wish for anything at all, I would wish for peace, happiness, and justice and equality for all persons, regardless of race."

WORLD WIDE WEB SITES:

http://www.achievement.org/autodoc/page/par0bio-1
http://memory.loc.gov/ammem/today/dec01.html
http://montgomery.troy.edu/rosaparks/museum
http://www.rosaparks.org
http://www.time.com/time/time100/heroes/profile/parks01.html

Colin Powell
1937 -
African-American Military Leader and Statesman
First African-American Secretary of State

COLIN POWELL WAS BORN April 5, 1937, in the Harlem section of New York City. His first name is pronounced COLE-in. His parents were Luther and Maud Powell. Luther and Maud were born in Jamaica and moved to the U.S. before Colin was born. Luther worked as a head of a shipping department and Maud worked as a seamstress. Colin has one sister, Marilyn, who is older.

COLIN POWELL GREW UP in the South Bronx section of New York. The family had moved there when Colin was six. It's now a very tough neighborhood. But when Powell was growing up it was the kind of place where grownups looked out for kids. It was a close community, with many different kinds of people. Powell remembers, "Jewish, mixed with Irish, Polish, Italian, black, and Hispanic families."

He had many relatives and close family friends who lived nearby. He remembers that it was a place "where everybody knows everybody's business, the same as in a small town."

Although he claims he wasn't "much of an athlete," he loved street games. Kids who grow up in cities don't always have parks to play in, so Colin and his friends played in the street when the traffic died down. He liked "stickball, stoopball, punchball, and sluggo." All those games were played without real baseballs, bats, and other expensive equipment. Instead, the kids used what they could find, like rubber balls and sticks.

COLIN POWELL WENT TO SCHOOL at the public schools in the South Bronx. He went to two elementary schools, P.S. 20 and P.S. 39. For junior high, he attended P.S. 52. His high school years were spent at Morris High.

He remembers that Morris "was a great school, but we didn't know it at the time. It was the school you went to when you couldn't get into one of the good schools. And I couldn't get into one of the smart schools because I had bad grades, terrible. Really, I'm not kidding. Bad grades all the way."

Powell graduated from Morris in 1955. He wasn't sure what he wanted to do with himself and decided to give college a try. At City College in New York, Powell studied geology. He was still just an average student, "with a straight-C average in my grades." But Powell got straight-As in ROTC.

ROTC is the "Reserve Officer Training Corps." It is a program that trains students to serve in the armed forces. It also pays for college for students who serve in the army after graduating. So after he graduated from City College, Powell started a career in the army.

LIFE AS AN ARMY OFFICER: Powell joined the army as a lieutenant (loo-TEN-ent). That is an officer rank. Officers are troop leaders. Powell served all over the world in a career that lasted 35 years. In the 1960s, he served in the Vietnam War. He was wounded twice, once while rescuing other soldiers. Powell also led troops in Korea and Europe. Powell loved the Army. "There was nothing else I ever wanted to do," he says. "And the beautiful part about the Army is that they were always giving me something that was beyond me. They were always testing me and they were always causing me to stretch."

Over the years, Powell continued to be recognized for his outstanding ability. He moved up from rank to rank to the highest position in the military: general. In 1989, he became a four-star general. He was the highest ranking African-American officer in U.S. history.

CHAIRMAN OF THE JOINT CHIEFS OF STAFF: In 1989, Colin Powell became Chairman of the Joint Chiefs of Staff. It is one of the most important jobs in the military. As Chairman, Powell was head of the chiefs of the Army, Navy, Air Force, and Marines. He was also the chief military adviser to the president.

THE GULF WAR: In 1990, the country of Iraq invaded the country of Kuwait. The U.S. became part of a military group that fought against Iraq to win freedom

Powell as Chairman of the Joint Chiefs of Staff.

for Kuwait. General Powell helped decide how the war should be fought. He worked in Washington and in the Middle East to help the U.S. forces to win against Iraq.

During his military career, Powell also worked in Washington, D.C. To date, he has served five U.S. presidents: Jimmy Carter, Ronald Reagan, George H.W. Bush, Bill Clinton, and George W. Bush.

RETIRING FROM THE ARMY: In 1993, Powell decided to retire from the military. Because he had been such a good leader, many people wanted him to run for President. Powell thought about the job. He wrote a book about his life, called *My American Journey*. As he traveled the country talking about his book, he talked with his fellow Americans. Many of them urged him to run.

Powell finally decided in the fall of 1995 that he would not run for President. He was especially concerned about his family. He thought they would have to make changes in their lives and lose their privacy.

AMERICA'S PROMISE: In 1997, Powell decided to take on another career. He started an organization called "America's Promise—the Alliance for Youth." It is an organization that helps improve the lives of young people. He wanted to reach kids who needed help. He wanted to give them five basic things he thinks every child needs. These are: an ongoing relationship with a caring adult, a safe place to learn and grow, a healthy start, a marketable skill, and a chance to serve others.

Because Powell is such a well-known figure, he's able to raise millions of dollars for the project. Companies gave money to connect schools to the Internet. Another company gave free eye exams and glasses to kids in the program.

Powell also wanted to find adult volunteers to help kids as mentors. In just a few years, he encouraged thousands of adults to help out. They act as tutors and in other ways to reach out and help kids. Powell is still active in the organization.

SECRETARY OF STATE: Powell entered government service again in 2000 when President George W. Bush nominated him to be Secretary of State. As a member of the President's Cabinet, Powell had to be approved by the U.S. Senate. And he was, with every Senator

Powell and his wife Alma are joined by former Presidents George H.W. Bush and Bill Clinton to celebrate the tenth anniversary of America's Promise Alliance in New York City, September 24, 2007.

voting to give him the job. He was the first African-American to hold the position.

As Secretary of State, Powell had many responsibilities. He was the President's chief advisor in foreign affairs. He negotiated treaties and agreements with other countries. He also handled negotiations between foreign countries. He was involved in major foreign policy decisions made by the Bush administration, especially after the 9/11 terrorist attacks. As head of the State Department, he was involved with issues ranging from war to immigration.

In January 2005, Powell decided to step down as Secretary of State. He's once again a private citizen, but is still consulted by government and military officials.

Powell and his wife, Alma, have devoted their time and money to charities for years. "Alma and I have been deeply involved in volunteer activities throughout our lives. All of us who have talent and time, and have been blessed with resources, should give back. It's a value that we should teach our children, particularly in the black community. So much has been given to us, so many opportunities are available to us that weren't available to earlier generations. We have an obligation to make the most of what's offered to us and to give back and to help others."

COLIN POWELL'S HOME AND FAMILY: Powell met his wife, Alma, in his early years in the army. They married in 1962. The Powells have three children, Michael, Linda, and Anne, and several grandchildren.

The Powells live outside of Washington, D.C. When he's not traveling or giving speeches, Powell likes to read, work on old cars, and play with his grandchildren.

HIS LEGACY: Powell has achieved several major milestones as an African-American leader. While he was in the military, he rose to become the highest ranking black officer in history. In government service, he became the first African-American Secretary of State. His legacy, of course, is not complete, and he will continue to add to a distinguished career of service to his country.

WORLD WIDE WEB SITES:

http://www.achievement.org/autodoc/page/pow0bio-1

http://goarmy.com/bhm/profiles-powell.jsp

http://www.whitehouse.gov/government/powell-bio.html

Condoleezza Rice
1954 -
African-American Secretary of State
First African-American Woman to
Serve as Secretary of State

CONDOLEEZZA RICE WAS BORN on November 14, 1954, in Birmingham, Alabama. Her parents were John Rice and Angelena Rice. Her father was a college administrator and minister and her mother taught music and science. She is an only child.

Her mother created her unusual name. Condoleezza (kahn-dah-LEE-za) is taken from an Italian musical term, "con dolcezza," meaning "with sweetness." She's always been known as "Condi" to her friends.

CONDOLEEZZA RICE GREW UP in a loving family that expected much of her. She started piano at age three. She began studying French and Spanish a few years later. She says her parents put her in "every book club," so she read a lot, too.

GROWING UP IN THE SEGREGATED SOUTH: Rice grew up in a segregated world. She lived in an all-black neighborhood and went to an all-black school. It was a time in American history when black people did not have the same rights as white people. Blacks could not buy houses or find jobs where they wanted. In the South, they couldn't use the same buildings as white people. Blacks had to use different restaurants, movie theaters, even drinking fountains.

During the **CIVIL RIGHTS MOVEMENT** of the 1960s, blacks became the targets of racial violence. And Birmingham, Alabama, was at the center of the struggle. In 1963, the 16th Avenue Baptist Church in Birmingham was bombed by white racists. Four girls died. One of them was a friend of Condi Rice. She recalled the tragedy later. "Birmingham was a violent place in 1963-64," she said. But Rice was taught to see beyond the violence born of racial hatred. "Our parents really did have us convinced that you couldn't have a hamburger at Woolworth's, but you could be President of the United States."

CONDOLEEZZA RICE WENT TO SCHOOL at the local public schools in Birmingham. She was an outstanding student. She skipped both first and seventh grades. When she was 14, the family moved to Denver. Her dad had gotten a job at the University of Denver.

Rice graduated from high school at age 14. She started college at the University of Denver at 15. At that time, she thought she would be a concert pianist. But she realized she didn't have the talent. "I was going to have to practice and practice and practice and was never going to be extraordinary," she says.

Then she took a class that changed her life. It was a course in international politics taught by a professor named Josef Korbel. He was a former diplomat from Czechoslovakia who had brought his family to the U.S. after World War II. Korbel was also the father of Madeleine Albright, who would go on to become the first woman Secretary of State. Rice was often a guest in the Korbel home.

Through Korbel, Rice discovered what would become her life's work. She took courses in Russian history, concentrating on the Soviet Union. After World War II, the Soviet Union and the U.S. became the two strongest nations in the world. They represented two very different political systems. The U.S. was a democracy. The Soviet Union was a Communist state. For more than 40 years, the hostilities between these two powers determined world politics.

It was this aspect of politics that fascinated Rice. She wanted to understand the nature of political power. "How it operates, how it's used," intrigued her, she says. She read all the books she could find on World War II, "and about war in general," she recalls.

Rice graduated with honors from the University of Denver in 1974. She went on to earn a master's degree from the University of Notre Dame in 1975. Rice returned to the University of Denver for

Rice, George W. Bush, and adviser Paul Wolfowitz at Bush's ranch in Crawford, Texas, before the 2000 Presidential election

her doctoral degree, which she completed in 1981. That same year, she became a professor at Stanford University.

FIRST JOBS: For the next 18 years, Rice rose within the ranks at Stanford. She worked as a professor of political science for several years. Her special areas were arms control and the Soviet Union.

Rice developed a reputation as a smart, hardworking scholar. She was considered brilliant and charming. But she also had "velvet-glove forcefulness," said Coit Blacker of Stanford. "She's a steel magnolia," he said. "She always knows what she wants and is extremely disciplined."

SERVING IN THE ADMINISTRATION OF GEORGE H.W. BUSH:
Rice's reputation brought her to the attention of President George

H.W. Bush, who was president from 1989 to 1993. She joined his administration in 1989 as assistant for national security affairs. She was also senior director for Soviet Affairs in the National Security Council.

George Bush was President at a time of great change in the world. During his term, the Soviet Union abandoned Communism and broke up into many independent states. The former Communist nations of Eastern Europe became democracies. This was the end of the "Cold War," the hostilities between the U.S. and the Soviets.

Now, a "new world order," as Bush called it, was at hand. It was a thrilling time to be part of world politics. Rice helped develop the U.S. response to changes taking place in Europe. When Bush met with Soviet leader Mikhail Gorbachev, he introduced her. "This is Condoleezza Rice," he said. "She tells me everything I know about the Soviet Union." Gorbachev said to Rice, "I hope you know a lot."

As an aide to Bush, Rice wasn't afraid of showing her "steel magnolia" side. She once blocked Russian leader Boris Yeltsin from entering an area of the White House. Yeltsin wanted to see Bush. Rice said no. Yeltsin backed down.

BACK TO STANFORD: After several years working for Bush, Rice returned to Stanford. In 1993, she became Provost of the university. A Provost is a high-ranking college administrator. Rice was the youngest person ever chosen for the job, as well as the first woman, and the first African-American. She determined budgets, developed curriculums, and handled a wide variety of issues.

Rice talks with Secretary of State Colin Powell,
June 2001.

SERVING IN THE ADMINISTRATION OF GEORGE W. BUSH: In 1999, Rice stepped down as Provost of Stanford. She became a close adviser of George W. Bush as he started his campaign for President.

Bush and Rice worked well together. Bush calls her the person who "can explain to me foreign policy matters in a way I can understand." He said she was a "good manager and an honest broker of ideas." She also became a close friend of the President and his family.

Rice helped Bush develop his foreign policy strategy during the campaign. She traveled with him, met with the press, and answered questions about Bush's stance on international issues.

Rice meets with President Bush, Vice President Cheney, and other officials following the terrorist attacks, September 15, 2001.

After he won the election in 2000, Bush chose Rice to be his national security adviser.

THE NATIONAL SECURITY ADVISER: The national security adviser is the chief consultant to the President on foreign policy. Rice was the first woman ever to hold the post. She advised the President on issues relating to foreign policy. She also discussed treaties between the U.S. and other nations. And she gave him advice in her special areas of interest, nuclear weapons and missile defense systems.

A TERRORIST ATTACK ON THE UNITED STATES: On September 11, 2001, terrorists attacked New York City and Washington. In her role as national security adviser, Rice played a pivotal role in determining U.S. policy after the attack. Together with the President, the Cabinet, and military officials, she helped plan America's response.

SECRETARY OF STATE: On January 26, 2005, Rice became Secretary of State. She became the first African-American woman ever to hold the job. She replaced **Colin Powell,** who stepped down from the position at the end of George W. Bush's first term.

As Secretary of State, Rice is the chief diplomat of the U.S. She works to develop U.S. foreign policy. She travels around the world, defining and carrying out that policy in other countries. She's also involved with programs to fight disease, such as stopping the spread of AIDS in Africa.

Rice's major political focus is the Middle East. She is actively involved in U.S. foreign policy as it affects the war in Iraq. She has brokered talks between Israel and the Palestinians, hoping to pave the way for peace in the region. She is involved in trying to prevent Iran from developing nuclear weapons. She has overseen talks between North Korea and other nations to stop pursuing nuclear power.

CONDOLEEZZA RICE'S HOME AND FAMILY: Rice, who is single, lives in the Washington, D.C. area. Despite her busy schedule, she takes time to continue to play the piano. She especially likes to play in small chamber groups.

While at Stanford, Rice founded the Center for a New Generation. It's an after-school academy for poor, underprivileged kids in East Palo Alto. It provides a positive atmosphere where kids can do homework and play safely.

Rice loves to exercise. "Exercise is a very high priority for me," she says. "I do some of my best thinking on the treadmill." She also loves to play tennis. After her years at Stanford, she's become a devoted fan of the school teams. She loves football especially, both college and pro. She's joked that someday she'd like to be head of the National Football League.

Rice is very religious. "I have a very, very, powerful faith in God," she says. "I'm a really religious person, and I don't believe that I was put on this earth to be sour, so I'm eternally optimistic about things."

HER LEGACY: It is too early to define Condoleezza Rice's legacy. After the next election, she will be free to stay in politics, or go back to work at a college, or into business. But as the first African-American woman to be Secretary of State, she is already a person of historical importance. *Forbes* magazine has called her the most powerful woman in the world. *Time* magazine named her one of the Top 100 world leaders. She will most likely add to her distinguished list of accomplishments in the years to come.

WORLD WIDE WEB SITES:

http://www.forbes.com/lists/2005/
http://www.state.gov/secretary
http://www.time.com/time/
http://www.whitehouse.gov/nsc/ricebio.html

Jackie Robinson
1919 - 1972
African-American Professional Baseball Player
First African-American to Play Major League Baseball

JACKIE ROBINSON WAS BORN on January 31, 1919, in Cairo, Georgia. His full name was Jack Roosevelt Robinson. His parents were Jerry and Mallie Robinson. He was the youngest of five children. He had three brothers, Edgar, Frank, and Mack, and one sister, Willa Mae.

JACKIE ROBINSON GREW UP in Pasadena, California. His father abandoned the family when Jackie was a baby. His mother packed up her children and moved from Georgia to California. There, she worked as a housekeeper to support them.

Robinson didn't remember the move to California. But he did remember his mother's courage. "I remember, even as a small boy, having a lot of pride in my mother. I thought she must have some kind of magic to be able to do all the things she did, to work so hard and never complain and to make us all feel happy."

The Robinson kids all lived by their mother's values. Jackie said she taught them "the importance of family unity, religion, and kindness toward others. Her great dream for us was that we go to school."

All the Robinson kids pitched in, too. Jackie had a paper route, and he sold hot dogs at nearby Rose Bowl stadium.

FACING RACISM: Mallie Robinson worked hard, saved her money, and was finally able to buy a house. It was in a mostly white section of Pasadena. The neighbors were racist and hostile. The Robinsons endured their racial taunts and prejudice.

According to Jackie's sister, Willa Mae, the neighbors finally came around. "And then we got to be real friends and all in the neighborhood. They found out we were human, too. The color didn't do anything to them."

JACKIE ROBINSON WENT TO SCHOOL at the local public schools. He did well in school, and was an outstanding athlete, too. He remembered that, "some of my classmates would share their lunches with me if I played on their team."

Jackie went to Cleveland Elementary and Washington Elementary in Pasadena. He went to Washington Junior High, and around that time, started to get into trouble. He joined a street gang, and was on the road to making some bad choices when two people stepped in. One was a minister, Karl Downs. The other was a neighbor, Carl Andersen. These two men told Jackie he was making a big mistake.

Robinson recalled that Carl Anderson made him see that "if I continued with the gang, it would hurt my mother as well as myself." Anderson convinced him that it took courage not to follow the crowd. "Courage and intelligence lay in being willing to be different," he learned. He quit the gang and channeled his energy into sports.

Robinson attended John Muir Technical High School, where he concentrated on athletics. He lettered in four sports: football, basketball, baseball, and track. After graduating from high school, he began classes at Pasadena Junior College. He was a sports standout again: quarterback of a championship football team, and a track and baseball star, too.

UCLA: After two years of junior college, Robinson transferred to UCLA (University of California Los Angeles). He'd been given a football scholarship, but he dominated in other sports, too. "I became the university's first four-letter man," he recalled. In football, basketball, baseball, and track, Robinson was a star.

But despite the wishes of his mother, Robinson didn't finish college. He wanted to make a living playing sports, but that door was closed to him. It is hard to believe in our era, where African-Americans are among the finest athletes on the finest teams in professional sports. But back then, blacks were banned from the major leagues.

Robinson was worried about his future. How would he make a living? "I was convinced that no amount of education would help a black man get a job," he recalled.

FIRST JOBS: After leaving college, Robinson worked briefly as an athletic director at a youth camp. Then, he moved to Hawaii and played semi-pro football. Returning to California, he worked for Lockheed, a major airplane manufacturer.

WORLD WAR II: In 1941, the U.S. entered World War II. Robinson was drafted and served in the Army from 1942 to 1944. Once again, he faced racism. He and several other recruits scored high marks on the Officer's Candidate School exam. But they weren't allowed to become officers, solely because they were black. It was only through the efforts of championship boxer Joe Louis that Robinson and other blacks were finally allowed to take officer's training. He became a second lieutenant in 1943.

The military was still segregated, and Robinson and other black soldiers still faced prejudice. When he tried playing sports, some teams wouldn't play against him, simply because he was black. Once, he faced a court-martial because he refused to go to the back of a military bus. The charges were later dropped, but Robinson left the Army deeply disappointed. Still, he never gave up. He knew he could make a difference, in sports and in the world.

THE NEGRO LEAGUES: When Robinson left the Army, he joined the Kansas City Monarchs. They were a team in the Negro Leagues.

Robinson in a Kansas City Monarchs uniform, 1945.

African-Americans weren't allowed to play in the all-white major leagues. The Negro Leagues contained some of the best players in the country, but they were limited in where they could play, and how much money they could make.

"JIM CROW" AND THE NEGRO LEAGUES: Robinson and all black baseball players faced other barriers, too. Racial segregation was widespread in America. Especially in southern states, a practice referred to as **"JIM CROW"** separated public facilities, such as restrooms and drinking fountains, into areas for white people and Negroes, as African-Americans were then usually called.

These facilities were supposed to be "separate but equal," but the facilities for blacks were miserably inadequate. Traveling for blacks was especially difficult. "The fatiguing travel wouldn't have been so bad if we could have had decent meals," Robinson recalled. "There was no hotel in many places we played. Sometimes there was a hotel for blacks which had no eating facilities. Some of the crummy eating joints wouldn't serve us at all."

Still, Robinson overcame those obstacles and established himself as one of the best players in the league. And he got noticed. A man named Branch Rickey had a plan. He wanted to integrate major league baseball. He was waiting for just the right person. He needed a man of talent, integrity, and the strength to face the pressure that was bound to confront the first black player in the major leagues. He found that man in Jackie Robinson.

INTEGRATING BASEBALL: Branch Rickey was the president of the Brooklyn Dodgers. He met with Jackie Robinson in August 1945 and outlined his plan. He wanted Robinson to start with the Montreal Royals, the minor league team of the Dodgers. From there, he would move up to the major leagues. "I was thrilled, scared, and excited. I was incredulous. Most of all, I was speechless," Robinson recalled.

Rickey was plain about what they faced. "There's virtually nobody on our side," he told Robinson. "No owners, no umpires, very few newspapermen. And I'm afraid that many fans will be hostile.

We'll be in a tough position. We can win only if we can convince the world that I'm doing this because you're a great ballplayer and a fine gentleman."

BREAKING THE COLOR BARRIER: Robinson was up to the challenge. In 1946 he signed a contract with the Dodgers and became a sensation. People all over the country were talking about the young player. Black Americans considered him a hero. Some fans, especially in the South, were angry and insulting.

Robinson was ready for what he knew would come his way. He would have to take "abuse, name-calling, rejection by fans and sportswriters and by fellow players not only on opposing teams but on his own. He had to be able to stand up in the face of merciless persecution and not retaliate." It was his fate, and he faced it with athletic power and personal dignity.

Robinson played his first year in the minor leagues in 1946. At first, he was nervous, but his strength and confidence grew. He drew in huge crowds wherever he played. He had to sit out some games, because some teams wouldn't let blacks play. Despite that, he finished his first season leading the league and helped the Royals become league champions.

THE MAJOR LEAGUES: In 1947, Rickey knew the time had come. He promoted Robinson to the majors. The first black player in major league baseball, Robinson wanted to show the world how much he belonged.

On April 15, 1947, Robinson walked onto Ebbets Field and into history. But he started out the season without his characteristic power. That caused fans and players to heap abuse on him. He was spit on and jeered; he even received death threats. On one occasion, Ben Chapman, manager of the Philadelphia Phillies, screamed racial insults at Robinson during a game. It took all the control he could muster, but Robinson wouldn't fight back.

A strange thing happened. When the fans saw what had happened, they were furious at Chapman. When Robinson's teammates saw what happened, they came together as a team like never before. They defended their player, and made him one of their own.

Branch Rickey said that it was Chapman's actions that "made Jackie a real member of the Dodgers." "When he poured out that abuse, he solidified and united 30 men," Rickey recalled. It proved to be a great season for a great player. Robinson's play helped the Dodgers reach the playoffs and win the pennant. He was named Rookie of the Year by *Sporting News*. And thousands of African-Americans could finally see a black player on the field.

Robinson had started a revolution in American sports. Other teams began to hire black players. And he ended his historic first season as "a member of a solid team. The Dodgers were a championship team because all of us had learned something."

In the 1948 season, Robinson played well again, batting and fielding like a champ. In 1949, he led the league in batting and stolen bases, and led his team to the World Series. They lost to the New York Yankees, but Robinson was a confirmed star. He won the Most Valuable Player award that year.

Robinson was also being recognized as a leader of African-Americans. He appeared before Congress to discuss Paul Robeson, an African-American musician who supported the Communist

*Robinson steals home plate during a game
against the Boston Braves, August 22, 1948.*

party. Robinson told the political leaders that black Americans loved their country. "But that doesn't mean that we're going to stop fighting race discrimination until we've got it licked," he told them. "It means that we're going to fight it all the harder because our stake in the future's so big."

In 1950, Robinson appeared in a movie based on his life. He also swung the bat with power, averaging .328. The team missed the playoffs, and got ready for the next year.

The 1951 season saw the Dodgers face the Giants in the pennant race. They lost to the Giants, despite Robinson's fine play all season. In fact, he had a batting average of over .300 from 1951 to 1953. In 1952 and 1953, the Dodgers went to the World Series, losing both years to the Yankees.

In 1955 Robinson and the Dodgers won the championship they so wanted and deserved. Once again, they had a great season. And finally, after a hard-fought seven games, they won the World Series. "It was one of the greatest thrills of my life," Robinson said.

RETIREMENT: After one last season with the Dodgers, Robinson retired from baseball in 1957. He took a job at the Chock Full O'Nuts coffee company. He also devoted time to politics, charities, and working for civil rights. He was a popular speaker around the country, and did work for the **NAAACP**. Robinson supported the mission of the organization and raised money on its behalf.

HALL OF FAME: In 1962, Robinson became the first African-American to be inducted into the Baseball Hall of Fame. Fans around the world were delighted with this great recognition.

In the late 1960s, Robinson's health began to fail. He had heart disease and diabetes, and they limited his life. In June 1972, his old team, now the Los Angeles Dodgers, held a ceremony to commemorate the 25th anniversary of his breaking of the color line. Later that year, Robinson threw the first pitch at the 1972 World Series. He died on October 24, 1972. He was 53 years old.

HIS LEGACY: Jackie Robinson is one of the most important African-Americans in our history. Through athletic excellence, dignity, and courage, he showed the country that the measure of a man can never be determined by the color of his skin.

On the 50th anniversary of his breaking of the color line, all the teams in major league baseball retired his number, 42, from all their rosters.

Time magazine chose Robinson as one of the most important people of the 20th century. The tribute to him was written by another baseball great and African-American legend, **Hank Aaron**. He wrote about Robinson's life and legacy. In closing, he said this:

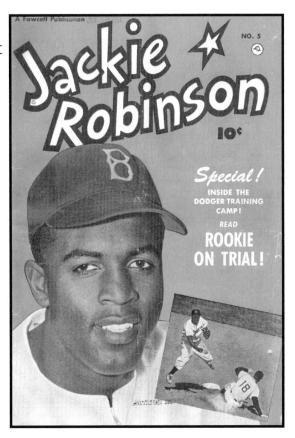

Front cover of a Jackie Robinson comic book, published in 1951.

"To this day, I don't know how he withstood the things he did without lashing back. I've been through a lot in my time, and I consider myself to be a patient man. But I know I couldn't have done what Jackie did. I don't think anybody else could have done it. Somehow, though, Jackie had the strength to suppress his instincts, to sacrifice his pride for his people's. It was an incredible act of selflessness that brought the races closer together than ever before and shaped the dreams of an entire generation."

JACKIE ROBINSON'S HOME AND FAMILY: Jackie Robinson met his future wife, Rachel Isum, when they were both students at UCLA. They married in 1946. Rachel was Jackie's ardent supporter throughout his life. They had three children, Jackie Jr., Sharon, and David.

WORLD WIDE WEB SITES:

http://espn.go.com/sportscentury/features/0016431.html

http://www.archives.gov/education/lessons/jackie-robinson/

http://www.jackierobinson.com

http://time.com/time/time100/heroes/profile/robinson01.html

Wilma Rudolph
1940 - 1994
African-American Track and Field Athlete
Winner of Three Olympic Gold Medals

WILMA RUDOLPH WAS BORN on June 23, 1940, in St. Bethlehem, Tennessee, about 50 miles from Nashville. Her full name was Wilma Glodean Rudolph. Her parents were Ed and Blanche Rudolph. Blanche worked as a maid. Ed worked as a porter for a railroad company, carrying suitcases for train passengers. He already had 11 children from his first marriage when he met Blanche. They had nine more children together. Wilma was one of the youngest members of this large family.

WILMA RUDOLPH GREW UP in the town of Clarksville, Tennessee. She was often sick as a child. When she was four years old, she caught polio. Polio is a virus that attacks the brain and spinal cord. It causes a high fever and sometimes paralysis (loss of movement). Polio damaged the nerves and muscles in Wilma's left leg. Her doctors worried that she might never be able to walk again.

Six-year-old Wilma Rudolph, right, poses with her older sister Yvonne.

Wilma wore a heavy metal brace on her leg for many years. Her mother and sisters rubbed her leg every day to make more blood flow to the muscles. One day each week, Wilma and her mother took a bus to Nashville. They went to a city hospital where Wilma learned exercises to strengthen her leg.

GROWING UP IN THE SEGREGATED SOUTH: During these weekly bus trips, Wilma saw the effects of segregation. At this time, segregation laws kept people in the South separated by race. Wilma and other African-Americans were forced to use different waiting areas, bathrooms, and drinking fountains than those used by white people. Black people also had to sit in the back of public buses.

When Wilma was nine years old, she shocked her doctors by walking without her leg brace. She wore special support shoes until she was 11. After that, she was completely healed. "By the time I was 12, I was challenging every boy in our neighborhood at running, jumping, everything," she remembered.

WILMA RUDOLPH WENT TO SCHOOL in Clarksville. Because of her illness, she did not start school until the second grade. She attended two all-black public schools, Cobb Elementary School and Burt High School. As she grew older, Wilma became a star basketball player. She averaged 32 points per game during her sophomore year of high school.

Wilma's speed on the court attracted the attention of Ed Temple. Temple was the women's track coach at Tennessee State University. He told Wilma that she had the talent to be a great runner. He invited her to train with his college team, the Tigerbelles, during the summer. The next year, Wilma joined her high school track team. She never lost a race in two seasons.

RUNNING IN THE 1956 OLYMPICS: Rudolph had never even heard of the Olympics until she met Ed Temple. She still managed to qualify for the 1956 Games in Melbourne, Australia. At 16, she was the youngest member of the U.S. team. Rudolph earned a bronze medal by helping the American women finish third in the 400-meter relay race. She knew at that time that she wanted to try for a gold medal in 1960.

*Rudolph winning the women's 100-meter dash at the
Rome Olympics, September 2, 1960.*

In 1958 Rudolph enrolled at Tennessee State. She studied education and joined the Tigerbelles track team. She practiced hard and qualified for three events at the 1960 Olympic Games in Rome, Italy.

1960 OLYMPICS: Rudolph's first event was the 100-meter sprint race. She won the gold medal easily, finishing three meters ahead of her closest competitor. A writer for *Time* magazine said that Rudolph's long, flowing strides "made the rest of the pack seem to be churning on a treadmill." Rudolph earned a second gold medal by winning the 200-meter race.

Then Rudolph joined three of her Tigerbelle teammates—Martha Hudson, Barbara Jones, and Lucinda Williams—in the 400-meter relay race. Each woman ran 100 meters and then passed a baton to the next woman. Rudolph ran the fourth, or anchor, leg of the race. When her turn came, she dropped the baton on the ground. But she picked it up and passed three other runners to claim a third gold medal. Rudolph became the first American woman ever to win three Olympic gold medals in track and field.

BECOMING A STAR: Rudolph's amazing performance at the 1960 Olympics made her a star in Europe and the United States. Many people were touched by the story of how she overcame illness, poverty, and segregation to become the world's fastest woman. Rudolph appeared in parades, gave interviews on television, and even visited President John F. Kennedy at the White House.

When Rudolph returned home to Tennessee, Clarksville officials organized a rally in her honor. But the event they planned was segregated. Rudolph refused to participate if only white people were invited. Town officials were forced to allow black people to attend. The rally attracted 40,000 people. It was the first racially integrated event in the town's history.

Now that she was famous, Rudolph found it hard to go back to her old life. But she could not earn a living as a track star. American companies did not hire black athletes to advertise their products in those days. Rudolph decided that she had to finish her education and get a job. She retired from track in 1963. She earned her college degree and started working as a teacher and coach.

Rudolph wins a gold medal in the women's 400-meter relay race at the Rome Olympics, September 8, 1960.

HELPING POOR CHILDREN ENJOY SPORTS: Rudolph learned many important lessons by competing in sports. She wanted to share her experiences with others. She also wanted to help more children from poor families get involved in sports. "My life wasn't like the average person who grew up and decided to enter the world of sports," she explained.

In 1977 Rudolph wrote a book about her life, called *Wilma*. It was turned into a TV movie starring Cicely Tyson and Denzel

Washington. Rudolph also gave speeches and helped open sports clinics in cities across the country. In 1981 she started the Wilma Rudolph Foundation to promote amateur sports. Rudolph always taught children the value of working hard to overcome the obstacles in their lives.

WILMA RUDOLPH'S HOME AND FAMILY: Rudolph was married and divorced twice. She had four children: daughters Yolanda and Djuanna, and sons Robert Jr. and Xurry. Rudolph died of a cancerous brain tumor at her home in Brentwood, Tennessee, on November 12, 1994. She was 54 years old.

HER LEGACY: Rudolph is a symbol of courage and perseverance to generations of athletes, black and white, male and female. She received many awards over the years for her achievements on and off the track. She was a member of the U.S. Olympic Hall of Fame, the National Track and Field Hall of Fame, and the Black Athletes Hall of Fame. Rudolph's image appeared on a U.S. postage stamp, and Tennessee State University named its new track after her. The Women's Sports Foundation created the Wilma Rudolph Courage Award in her honor. It is presented each year to a female athlete who succeeds in the face of challenges. "The triumph can't be had without the struggle," she said. "And I know what struggle is. I have spent a lifetime trying to share what it has meant to be a woman first in the world of sports so that other young women have a chance to reach their dreams."

WORLD WIDE WEB SITES:

http://www.wilmarudolph.net
http://www.lkwdpl.org/wihohio/rudo-wil.htm
http://espn.go.com/sportscentury/features/00016444.html

Bill Russell
1934 -
African-American Basketball Player, Coach,
Commentator, and Author
First African-American Coach in the NBA
First African-American Inducted into the
NBA Hall of Fame

BILL RUSSELL WAS BORN on February 12, 1934, in Monroe, Louisiana. His full name when he was born was William Felton Russell. His parents were Charles and Katie Russell. Charles worked in a factory that made paper bags. Bill had a brother named Charles.

BILL RUSSELL GREW UP in Louisiana until he was nine, when the family moved to Oakland, California. Both Bill's father and mother found work in a factory that made supplies for the military.

Life in California was not much better for the Russell family. In the early years they lived in an eight-room house shared by eight other families. Mr. Russell started a small trucking company, and the family could afford to move to a housing project.

Then, tragedy struck the family. Bill's mother died at the age of 32. Charles Russell worked hard to raise his sons alone. He went to work in a metal foundry. After work, he was home teaching his sons how to live their lives properly. Russell said later of his father, "He was always a man. He raised us by himself, and he taught us to be men, no matter what."

BILL RUSSELL WENT TO SCHOOL in both Louisiana and California. In Louisiana, he attended an all-black school that was a converted barn. In Oakland, he attended the public schools.

Bill reached his teen years as an ungainly and thin youngster, not yet a basketball power. He attended all-black McClymonds High School. He didn't make the basketball team as a freshman. As a sophomore, he only played as a reserve. He even had to share a uniform with a teammate.

Russell's coach saw his potential, and encouraged him. He remembers that coach with gratitude. "I believe that man saved me from becoming a juvenile delinquent. If I hadn't had basketball, all my energies and frustrations would surely have been carried in some other direction."

Russell practiced at school and at the local Boys' Club. As he grew older, he gained weight and muscle, adding power and precision to his game.

As a senior, Russell starred on the McClymonds' team at center. His play earned him a basketball scholarship to the University of San Francisco (USF). The school was small, and didn't even have a gym of its own. Russell later told a reporter, "I had been living across San Francisco Bay most of my life, and I didn't even know there was a university there." But he was grateful for the scholarship. "I couldn't have gone to college any other way," he said.

COLLEGE: Russell started at USF in 1953. His roommate was another basketball player and a future Boston Celtics teammate, K.C. Jones. The two together, with Jones at guard and Russell at center, put USF on the college basketball map.

The school was an unknown, but in 1955 and 1956 USF won back-to-back NCAA basketball championships. In one streak they won 55 straight games, and were ranked as the top college team in the country. With this new-found success, USF decided to build their own basketball arena. Russell was named a first-team All-American player in his junior and senior years.

Russell's height and strength made him a great high-jumper, too. He almost broke a world record while a member of the USF track team. Russell graduated from USF in 1956.

THE 1956 OLYMPICS: Russell played in the 1956 Olympic Games in Melbourne, Australia. They had a record of 8–0, and defeated the U.S.S.R. for the gold-medal. Russell returned from

Russell (6) in a game against the St. Louis Hawks, February 1957.

Australia with great expectations for a professional career in basketball.

NBA: In the mid-1950s black players were still rare in the National Basketball Association (NBA). But Russell was of interest to every team in the league. Red Auerbach of the Boston Celtics traded two of his players to get Russell.

THE BOSTON CELTICS: Russell became a Celtic, with a starting salary of $19,500. He went on to have one of the finest careers in pro ball. When he joined the team, the Celtics had never won an NBA championship. When he left the team, they'd won 11 titles.

WINNING RINGS AND BUILDING A DYNASTY: Bill Russell and the Celtics, under Auerbach's coaching and with other strong players, won their first NBA title in 1957. In 1959, with Russell as their star center, the Celtics started an unmatched streak of eight straight titles from 1959 through 1966.

Russell was a champion from his first year. He changed the character of the Celtic team and the game, leading by example, and showing that strong defense was the key to a winning tradition.

Russell didn't make his name as a high scorer or shot maker. Instead, he played tight defense and became a top shot blocker. He was known for precision passing, handing off the ball to his teammates. "Shooting is of relatively little importance in a player's overall game," he said. He was also an intelligent student of the game. He could visualize defenses, and he knew the abilities and weaknesses of other teams.

THE RIVALRY: Russell played his entire career matched up against the other great NBA center of the time, Wilt Chamberlain. The two great centers were rivals on the court, and fought epic battles under the boards. Over the years, Chamberlain outscored and out-rebounded Russell. But when it came to winning, Russell came out on top. Russell's team beat Chamberlain's 86 to 57. Russell won nine NBA championships; Chamberlain only one.

Off the court, the two big men were good friends and had enormous respect for each other. As a sort of personal joke and friendly gesture of respect, they referred to each other by their middle names. Russell called Chamberlain "Norman." Chamberlain called Russell "Felton."

Russell is congratulated by coach Arnold "Red" Auerbach
after scoring his 10,000th point in a game
against the Baltimore Bullets, December 12, 1964.

Sports writer Mike Lupica called the Russell–Chamberlain rivalry the greatest individual competition in sports. "They battled each other with strength and skill and pride. They will forever be linked in the history of the sport."

FACING RACISM: Russell's years in the NBA weren't without their racist challenges. He played on the Celtics with some of the finest African-American players of the era, including K.C. Jones, Sam Jones, and Satch Sanders. In 1961, they were supposed to play a game in Lexington, Kentucky. But they were denied service at an Indiana bar and a Kentucky restaurant. They boycotted the game.

Russell was outspoken about racism in America. "The basic problem with the Negro in America is the destruction of race pride. One could say we have been victims of psychological warfare. This is a white country, and all the emphasis is on being white."

Throughout his career, Russell supported the **CIVIL RIGHTS MOVEMENT**. He charged the NBA with limiting the opportunities for African-American players. In the early 1960s, he traveled to the South to hold basketball clinics for black and white players. It was a dangerous thing for an African-American to do. At that time, civil rights demonstrators were being harassed and beaten. But Russell wouldn't compromise his beliefs.

BECOMING THE FIRST BLACK COACH IN THE NBA: Red Auerbach retired as head coach of the Celtics after the 1966 season. He moved to the Celtics management, and chose Russell as player-coach. Russell became the first black head coach in the history of the NBA. Russell's teams won the NBA titles in 1968 and 1969, their 10th and 11th titles. He decided to retire after the 1969 season.

RECORD STATS: Russell racked up some incredible statistics in his years with the Celtics. He was voted Most Valuable Player (MVP) five times. He led the league in rebounds four times. His career total of 21,620 was second only to his rival, Wilt Chamberlain (23,924). He averaged 15 points a game, in 963 games.

A COMPLEX CHARACTER: Russell wasn't like other players in many ways. He refused to sign autographs. He said "You owe the public the same thing it owes you. Nothing." He didn't

Player-coach Russell attempts to score against legendary rival,
Wilt Chamberlain, in a game between the Celtics and the L.A. Lakers, 1969.

attend the ceremony at the Boston Garden when they retired his number. When he became the first African-American inducted into the Basketball Hall of Fame, he didn't go to the awards.

FIRST RETIREMENT: In 1969 Russell retired from the Celtics. He was honored as one of the greatest players in the history of the NBA. In 1970 he became a TV commentator for NBC.

BACK TO BASKETBALL: Russell decided to return to the game in the late 1970s. He coached the Seattle SuperSonics from 1973 to 1977, and led them to the playoffs for the first time.

RETIREMENT, NUMBER TWO: In 1977, Russell returned to broadcasting, this time with CBS. His work as a basketball commentator was professional, insightful, and entertaining. He showed a deep understanding of the inner workings of the game. Fans loved his wisdom, and his great sense of humor.

MORE CAREER CHANGES: Russell left broadcasting in 1983. He returned to basketball in 1987, as coach of the Sacramento Kings. He had a very disappointing year as a head coach, and left the Kings after two years. It was the only setback in his professional career.

BILL RUSSELL'S HOME AND FAMILY: Russell married Rose Swisher in 1956. They had three children, Jacob, Karen Kenyatta, and William, Jr. They divorced in 1973. Later, Russell was briefly married to Didi Anstett.

HIS LEGACY: Bill Russell is considered one of the finest basketball players of all time. The first African-American to coach an

NBA team, and the first inducted into the Basketball Hall of Fame, he is honored as an athlete and a leader. "I played because I enjoyed it," he said. "But there's more to it than that. I played because I was dedicated to being the best. I was part of a team, and I dedicated myself to making that team the best."

WORLD WIDE WEB SITES:

http://espn.go.com/sportscentury/features/
http://www.nba.com/history/players/russell

Sojourner Truth
1797(?) - 1883
African-American Abolitionist and Activist

SOJOURNER TRUTH WAS BORN around 1797 in Ulster, New York. She was born a slave. Her name when she was born was Isabella Bomefree. (She chose the name "Sojourner Truth" later, when she became an activist.)

Her parents were James and Betsy Bomefree. They were slaves, and belonged to a Dutch immigrant named Hardenbergh. Isabella had 10 to 12 sisters and brothers. Each of them was sold into slavery when they were small. Her earliest memories were of her parents' overwhelming grief over the loss of their children.

The first language Isabella spoke was Dutch. Later, when she learned English, she still spoke with a Dutch accent.

LIFE AS A SLAVE: Over the first 30 years of her life, Isabella was owned by four men. In 1806, when she was only nine, she was taken from her parents and sold to an Englishman named John Nealy. She worked for him for about two years. She was sold again in 1808 to Martinus Schrynver. Two years later, she was sold again, to John Dumont.

Isabella worked for Dumont on his farm in New Paltz, New York, for 17 years. During those years, she married a man named Thomas, who was also a slave. They had five children. To her great horror, her son Peter was illegally sold to an Alabama slaveholder. She was determined to find him.

FREEDOM: The state of New York abolished slavery on July 4, 1827. Dumont promised Isabella that he would free her one year early, in 1826. But he went back on his word. Isabella was furious.

In late 1826, Isabella escaped to freedom. She was only able to take her baby daughter, Sophia, with her. "I did not run off, for I thought that wicked," she later claimed. "I walked off, believing that to be right."

Maria and Isaac Wagener, who lived in nearby Wagondale, took Isabella and Sophia in. She worked for them for several years, as a domestic employee.

Isabella began to search for Peter. She found him in Alabama, then sued his owner for his return. She became the first black

Truth presents President Abraham Lincoln with a Bible from the African-Americans of Baltimore, October 29, 1864.

woman in history to sue a white man, and win. Peter was joyfully reunited with his mother. They moved to New York City in 1829.

A WOMAN OF DEEP CHRISTIAN FAITH: Isabella became a devout Christian. She said that God appeared to her in a vision. She remembered being "overwhelmed with the greatness of the Divine presence." She believed she was called to preach the Gospel.

Isabella joined a religious group headed by a man named Elijah Pierson. He believed he was a prophet. Isabella worked for him, and preached with him. Another member of the group was a fiery speaker named Matthias. Matthias believed he was God.

When Pierson died under mysterious circumstances, Matthias was accused of his murder. Though she was innocent, Isabella was also charged. She was cleared of all charges, but she decided to leave New York. She wanted to pursue her calling on her own. She helped Peter find a job on a whaling ship, then became a traveling preacher.

BECOMING SOJOURNER TRUTH: In 1843, at the age of 46, Isabella changed her name to Sojourner Truth. She explained that she received the name from God. "My name was Isabella. But when I left the house of bondage, I left everything behind. I went to the Lord and asked him to give me a new name. And the Lord gave me Sojourner, because I was to travel up and down the land, showing the people their sins, and being a sign unto them."

For the next 40 years, Truth traveled the country as a preacher and activist. She was devoted to the cause of **ABOLITION** and women's rights. Abolitionists wanted to "abolish," or end, slavery in the country. In 1844, she joined a group in Northampton, Massachusetts, called the Northampton Association of Education and Industry. It was a community devoted to abolition. The group supported itself and its mission by raising and selling farm goods.

At Northampton, Sojourner met **Frederick Douglass** and William Lloyd Garrison. They encouraged her to speak and continue to fight against slavery. She also met Olive Gilbert. Gilbert was devoted to abolition and women's rights, too. Sojourner couldn't read or write. So Gilbert helped her complete her autobiography. *The Narrative of Sojourner Truth: A Northern Slave* was first published by William Garrison in 1850. The book provided an income for Truth, and she was able to buy a house in Northampton.

The book helped make Sojourner a well-known and respected speaker. She traveled the country speaking out against slavery and for women's rights. She often spoke of her own life, and listeners were moved by her straightforward, uncompromising vision. One of her speeches is still studied today.

"AIN'T I A WOMAN?" On May 29, 1851, Truth gave her most famous speech at a women's rights convention in Ohio. One speaker claimed that women were too weak to be able to vote. Truth's response has thundered across the ages. "That man over there says women need to be helped into carriages, and lifted over ditches," she said. "Nobody ever helps me into carriages, or over mud-puddles, or gives me any best place! And ain't I a woman? Look at me! I have plowed and planted, and gathered into barns, and no man could head me! And ain't I a woman? I could work as much, and eat as much as a man—when I could get it—and bear the lash as well! And ain't I a woman?"

In 1853, Truth met Harriet Beecher Stowe. Stowe was the author of *Uncle Tom's Cabin*. That famous novel spelled out the evils of slavery, and inflamed the nation. Stowe wrote about Truth in the *Atlantic Monthly* magazine. Truth's fame continued to grow.

In 1857, Truth moved from Massachusetts to Michigan. She lived with a community of Quakers who worked for abolition, women's rights, and nonviolence. As the country headed toward Civil War, Truth continued to travel and to speak.

When the Civil War began in 1861, Truth rallied African-Americans to join the cause. She spoke to black soldiers and encouraged others to join. She was proud that her grandson James served in the honored 54th Regiment from Massachusetts. That unit was made up of all African-American volunteers. It also included two of Frederick Douglass's sons.

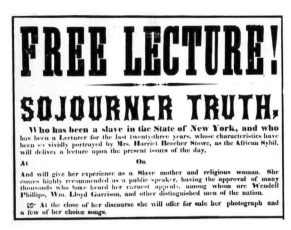

Newspaper announcement for one of Truth's lectures.

During the war, Truth met with President Abraham Lincoln. She presented him with a Bible from the freed blacks of Baltimore. The scene of their meeting became a famous painting. (See the painting in this entry.)

WORK ON BEHALF OF FREEDMEN AND WOMEN: After the Civil War ended in 1865, Truth worked for the betterment of black Americans. She worked for the Freedman's Relief Association. As part of that group, she helped former slaves to begin lives as free people. She worked in the Freedman's Hospital in Washington, D.C.

Almost 100 years before **Rosa Parks,** Truth filed a lawsuit to desegregate public transportation. She wanted black people to be able to ride on the streetcars of Washington, D.C. She won her case. She also spoke before Congress. She wanted the government to grant land to former slaves in the West. They gave her a standing ovation, but didn't approve her proposal.

Truth also continued to travel and speak all over the country. Well into her 80s, she spoke in support of women's rights and temperance (the banning of alcohol). She tried to vote in the Presidential election of 1872, but wasn't allowed to.

Finally, Truth's health began to fail. She died on November 26, 1883, at her home in Battle Creek, Michigan. She was 86 years old. There is a memorial and institute in Battle Creek that celebrate her many achievements.

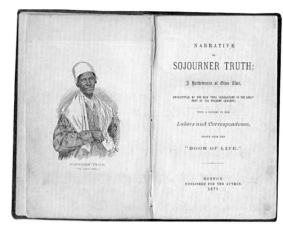

Title page of Truth's autobiography.

SOJOURNER TRUTH'S HOME AND FAMILY: Truth married a man named Thomas while she lived on the Dumont farm. They had five children. Four survived to be adults. Those four were Diana, Peter, Elizabeth, and Sophia. Peter was most likely lost at sea in the 1840s. Diana and Elizabeth and their families lived with their mother in Battle Creek until the end of her life.

HER LEGACY: Sojourner Truth was a woman of strength, determination, and courage. She overcame the horrors of slavery to become a tireless advocate for African-Americans and women. With passion and the promise of freedom for the oppressed, she truly "spoke Truth to Power."

WORLD WIDE WEB SITES:

http://www.lkwdpl.org/wihohio/trut-soj.htm
http://www.sojournertruth.org
http://www.sojournertruthmemorial.org

Harriet Tubman
1820? - 1913
African-American Abolitionist and Activist
Conductor of the Underground Railroad

HARRIET TUBMAN WAS BORN around 1820 in Dorchester County, Maryland. She was born a slave. Her name when she was born was Araminta Ross. Her parents were Ben and Harriet Ross. She changed her first name to Harriet in honor of her mother. Her parents were both slaves. Harriet was one of 11 children. Despite their plight as slaves, Ben and Harriet Ross loved and protected their children. They raised them all to have a deep Christian faith.

LIFE AS A SLAVE: When she was about five years old, Harriet began to work as a house slave. Her master hired her out to help another slave owner as a nursemaid. Only a child herself, Harriet was beaten if she fell asleep, or if the baby in her care cried. When she was about 12, she was sent to work in the fields. The work was brutally hard. So was the overseer's treatment of the slaves.

One day Harriet tried to save a fellow slave from a beating by the overseer. The overseer threw a heavy rock, and it struck Harriet. The blow nearly killed her. She suffered from seizures the rest of her life.

In 1844, Harriet married a free black man named John Tubman. She continued to live as a slave. By 1849, Harriet feared she might be sold. She made a decision to run away.

ESCAPING TO FREEDOM: In 1849, Tubman fled Maryland and slavery. Her husband refused to come with her. Guided by the North Star, she made her way to Philadelphia, where she was finally free. "I had crossed the line of which I had so long been dreaming," she said. But she missed her family. She was determined to rescue them from slavery and bring them to the North.

Tubman found work as a cook in Philadelphia. As soon as she had enough money, she arranged to help her sister and her sister's children to escape to freedom. Over the next several years, she brought her entire family to the North, and to freedom.

BECOMING A CONDUCTOR ON THE UNDERGROUND RAIL-ROAD: Through freeing her family members, Tubman met many other slaves who wanted to escape. She joined what is called the **UNDERGROUND RAILROAD**. It was a secret network of roads and

*This lithograph, entitled "Underground Railroad," depicts
African-Americans escaping slavery.*

safe houses, where slaves could stay on their route to the North.
The "railroad" led all the way to northern New York and into
Canada.

Tubman met William Still, the station master for Philadelphia.
He was an important organizer of the Underground Railroad. He
helped Tubman learn the system of the "Railroad."

Tubman became a "conductor." That meant that she organized
and led groups of slaves to freedom. It was dangerous work, but
she was fearless. There were large rewards for her capture, as both
a runaway slave and a "conductor."

Tubman insisted that the slaves in her care follow her rules.
She carried a rifle at all times. She threatened to use it against any

slave who wanted to return to slavery. But she never wavered in her work. And she never lost a single person. "On my Underground Railroad I never ran my train off the track, and I never lost a passenger," she recalled.

"THE MOSES OF HER PEOPLE": Over the span of 16 years, Tubman led over 300 slaves to freedom. As Moses in the Bible led the Israelites from bondage in Egypt, she led her people to freedom. For this, she became known as "The Moses of Her People."

Through her work, she met some of the most important **ABOLITIONISTS** of her time. (Abolitionists wanted to "abolish," or end, slavery in the country.) She met **Frederick Douglass** and John Brown. Douglass said, "Excepting John Brown, I know of no one who has willingly encountered more perils and hardships to serve our enslaved people than Harriet Tubman."

Another important friend was William H. Seward. He was a prominent abolitionist and Republican from Auburn, New York. Seward championed Tubman, and helped her buy a home in Auburn. He was also Lincoln's Secretary of State as the nation entered the Civil War.

THE ELECTION OF ABRAHAM LINCOLN: Abraham Lincoln was elected President in 1860. He was the candidate of the Republican Party. That party had been formed by people who were opposed to slavery in the new territories. The Southern states knew that a vote for Lincoln was a vote against slavery. Two months after the election, seven Southern states "seceded" from the Union. That means that they chose to no longer be a part of the United States. Instead, they formed their own new country, called the Confederate States of America.

THE CIVIL WAR: The national argument over slavery led the nation to Civil War in 1861. The war lasted four years, and losses on both sides were horrific. Tubman continued to play an important part in her nation's cause. She served as a nurse, a soldier, and a spy for the Union.

NURSE: In 1862, Tubman was sent to Beaufort, South Carolina, to nurse soldiers. She also helped the new black freedman to learn to make a living on their own. But her work in South Carolina included other, more dangerous, assignments.

A SPY FOR THE UNION: Tubman led a group of former slaves on a scouting mission. They prepared reports on the location of Confederate camps for the Union. These aided the invasion of South Carolina led by Colonel James Montgomery. Tubman served as a soldier for Montgomery, too. In 1863, Tubman and 150 black soldiers took part in a gunboat raid in South Carolina.

SETTLING IN AUBURN, NEW YORK: After the war, Tubman moved to Auburn, New York. She married a soldier she'd met in the war, Nelson Davis. She decided to devote herself to the care of children and the elderly. She also became involved in the fight for women's rights.

WOMEN'S RIGHTS ACTIVIST: Tubman met many of the prominent members of the women's rights movement. Susan B. Anthony and Elizabeth Cady Stanton became her friends and fellow activists. Tubman was a delegate to the National Federation of Afro-American Women's first meeting in 1896.

Portrait of Harriet Tubman taken in 1911.

BUILDING THE HARRIET TUBMAN HOME: Tubman bought 25 acres of land near her home in Auburn. On that property, she built the Harriet Tubman Home for Aged and Indigent Colored People. It became home to many of the area's poor and elderly blacks.

Although she had been a hero of the abolitionist movement and the Civil War, Tubman didn't receive any money for her services until the 1890s. She died in the home she had created on March 10, 1913, at the age of 93. She was buried in Auburn with military honors.

HARRIET TUBMAN'S HOME AND FAMILY: Tubman was married twice. Her first husband was John Tubman. He and Harriet married in 1844. From 1849 until the Civil War, Harriet helped all of her family escape to the North. When she returned for John, he had married another woman. After the Civil War, Tubman married again. Her second husband was named Nelson Davis.

HER LEGACY: Tubman was a woman of incredible courage and devotion to the cause of freedom. Yet this champion of civil rights rarely received the honors she surely deserved. "I have wrought in the day—you in the night," wrote Frederick Douglass to Tubman. "I have had the applause of the crowd and the satisfaction that comes of being approved by the multitude. The most that you have done has been witnessed by a few trembling, scarred, and footsore bondsmen and women, whose heartfelt "God bless you' has been your only reward."

In recent years, Tubman's achievements have been more widely recognized. Her Auburn home is now a state historical site. In 1995, the U.S. Post Office honored her with a commemorative stamp. And in 2003, the Governor of New York declared March 10th "Harriet Tubman Day."

WORLD WIDE WEB SITES:

http://www.americaslibrary.gov/cgi-bin/page.cgi/aa/tubman
http://www.nyhistory.com/harriettubman.life.htm
http://www/pbs.org/wgbh/aia/

Booker T. Washington
1856 - 1915
African-American Educator and Political Leader
Founder of the Tuskegee Institute

BOOKER T. WASHINGTON WAS BORN in 1856, in Hale's Ford, Virginia. He was born a slave. Because he was a slave, no record of his exact birth date exists. His name when he was born was Booker Taliaferro. He was born on the tobacco plantation of a man named James Burroughs.

Booker's mother's name was Jane. She was a slave, and the plantation cook. His father was a white man. Booker never knew anything more about him than that. His mother later married another slave named Washington Ferguson, who became Booker's stepfather.

BOOKER T. WASHINGTON GREW UP on the Burroughs farm. His life was incredibly difficult. As a small child, he worked as hard as most adults. "There was no period of my life that was devoted to play," he remembered.

When Washington was growing up, it was against the law to educate slaves. He longed to learn to read and write. One of his tasks as a slave was to carry the books of one of the Burroughs's daughters to school. That experience only made him want to learn even more. "I had the feeling that to get into a schoolhouse and study would be about the same as getting into paradise," he recalled.

Washington's life, and the life of all African-Americans, was about to change.

THE ELECTION OF ABRAHAM LINCOLN: Abraham Lincoln was elected President in 1860. He was the candidate of the Republican Party. That party had been formed by people who were opposed to slavery in the new territories of the U.S. The Southern states knew that a vote for Lincoln was a vote against slavery. Two months after the election, seven Southern states "seceded" from the Union. That means that they chose to no longer be a part of the United States. Instead, they formed their own new country, called the Confederate States of America.

THE CIVIL WAR: The Civil War lasted from 1861 to 1865. The battles of the war were fought in several states, including Virginia,

Washington in a portrait taken between 1880 and 1890.

Mississippi, Pennsylvania, and Tennessee. Some of the fiercest and most decisive battles took place at Bull Run, Antietam, Chancellorsville, Vicksburg, and Gettysburg. The loss of life was terrible. All together, more than 300,000 people died in the Civil War.

THE EMANCIPATION PROCLAMATION: On January 1, 1863, Lincoln issued "The Emancipation Proclamation." It said that all slaves living in Confederate states were free.

During the war, Booker's stepfather, Washington Ferguson, escaped and fled to Malden, West Virginia. When the war ended in 1865, Booker, his mother, and other siblings left to join his stepfather.

LIFE AS A FREE BLACK: Booker was just nine years old when the war ended. He looked forward to freedom and going to school. But first he had to prove himself to his stepfather. His stepfather insisted that Booker work in the salt mines, then in the local coal mines.

It was back-breaking work. But Booker did it, because his stepfather had said that if he worked every day, he could go to school.

EDUCATION—AT LAST: Booker's first schooling began when he was ten. He started each day in the mines at 4 a.m. Then, he went to school. He attended the local school for black children for several years. When he started school, he took his father's first name, Washington, as his last name.

When he was about 15, Washington became a houseboy for a wealthy family, the Ruffners. Mr. Ruffner owned the mines. Mrs. Ruffner encouraged Washington's desire to learn.

Washington finished primary school at 16. He was determined to go to college. The same year he finished primary school, he walked nearly 500 miles, from Malden to Virginia, to enroll in Hampton Institute. It was a college founded to educate former slaves.

Washington at work in his office at the Tuskegee Institute

When Washington arrived, he was dirty and in ragged clothes. The head teacher wasn't sure what to make of him. She made him clean a room, then admitted him.

Washington spent the next four years at Hampton. He was an outstanding student and believed deeply in the school's mission: to train "the head, the hand, and the heart." The "head" represented academic preparation. The "hand" stood for learning manual labor. And the "heart" stressed the importance of service and faith. He would remember those values later, when he founded his own school. To help pay for college, Washington worked as a janitor.

FIRST JOBS: After graduating with honors from Hampton in 1875, Washington moved back to Malden. He taught school there for a few years. Next, he moved to Washington, D.C. and studied religion. But Washington wanted to teach, and returned to Hampton as a college teacher.

Washington taught at Hampton from 1879 to 1881. That year, he was given an opportunity that would make him a famous and honored man.

FOUNDING THE TUSKEGEE INSTITUTE: The state of Alabama had asked the president of Hampton, Samuel Chapman Armstrong, to help them find the head of a new school. They wanted to start a "vocational," school for African-Americans. That is, they wanted a school that would teach trades, like carpentry, shoemaking, and farming. The school would be in Tuskegee, Alabama. Armstrong recommended Washington. Only 25 years old, Washington took the job.

Washington moved to Tuskegee, only to find out that there were no buildings, and only $2,000 in funding. He had to find teachers, students, and money. He had to design courses and plan and direct the building of the campus.

Washington worked tirelessly. He led the students in the building of the new college. They made bricks, constructed the buildings, and built the Tuskegee Institute together. He hired outstanding faculty, including **George Washington Carver**. Carver led the agriculture department. He shared his new farming techniques with a generation of freed blacks. He helped to improve the lives of African-Americans throughout the South.

*The faculty of Tuskegee Institute with philanthropist
Andrew Carnegie, seated next to Washington, 1906.*

Washington stressed practical education. Tuskegee taught academic courses. But the school also prepared students to be carpenters, brick layers, and farmers. He encouraged black female students to learn "home economics." That's the study of homemaking. Washington believed that freed blacks needed these kinds of basic skills so that they could go out into the world and make a living. He also encouraged his students to share their learning with other blacks, to improve their way of life. And he always stressed the importance of religion and going to church.

A LEADING EDUCATOR AND POLITICAL FIGURE: Washington led Tuskegee for 34 years. He became an honored educator. Washington wrote a famous autobiography, *Up from Slavery*. In it, he detailed his stirring life story.

Portrait of Margaret Murray,
Mrs. Booker T. Washington

Washington was much admired throughout the country. He was able to gain financial help from wealthy white business people, like Andrew Carnegie. (He was one of the richest industrialists of his day.) That helped Washington further his work at Tuskegee.

A FAMOUS SPEECH: Washington became the most influential black leader in America. On September 18, 1895, he gave a famous speech at the Atlanta Exposition. He was so popular at the time that the speech was national news.

Washington talked about how the black and white races should work together in America. He wanted whites to give blacks more opportunity. He also said that "in all things purely social we can be as separate fingers, yet one as the hand in all things essential to mutual progress."

OPPOSING VIEWS: Some black leaders disagreed with Washington's ideas. They thought he tried too hard to be acceptable to white people. They thought Washington was too willing to accept what white people defined as the "place" of black people. And they thought his description of the races as being "separate fingers" indicated that Washington approved of segregation.

Booker T. Washington and his family.

Washington believed that as long as blacks worked hard and were patient, equal rights would be theirs. But that was not to be. Racial discrimination and violence against blacks continued to grow. Many prominent black leaders, including **W. E. B. Du Bois** challenged Washington's beliefs. They thought that only through political and social struggle could equality be achieved.

By the end of his life, Washington had changed his mind. He could see that his belief in progress through hard work and education had failed to achieve racial equality. The fight for Civil Rights would be carried on by others, with other means and beliefs.

BOOKER T. WASHINGTON'S HOME AND FAMILY: Washington was married three times. He and his first wife, Fannie N. Smith, were married in 1882. Fannie died two years later. Washington and his second wife, Olivia A. Davidson, married in 1885. She died in 1889. In 1893, Washington married Margaret James Murray. They had three children, Booker T. Jr., Ernest Davidson, and Portia Marshall.

Booker T. Washington died on November 14, 1915, in Tuskegee. He was 59 years old. He is buried on the campus of what is now Tuskegee University.

HIS LEGACY: Though still controversial to some, Washington is remembered as a tireless advocate for African-Americans. On the campus of Tuskegee, there is a monument to him, called "Lifting the Veil." The inscription reads: "He lifted the veil of ignorance from his people and pointed the way to progress through education and industry."

WORLD WIDE WEB SITES:

http://memory.loc.gov/ammem/aachtml/exhibit/
http://www.historycooperative.org/btw/info.html
http://www.nps.gov/archive/bowa/btwbio.html
http://www.tuskegee.edu/global/story/

Ida B. Wells
1862 - 1931
African-American Journalist and Activist

IDA B. WELLS WAS BORN on July 16, 1862, in Holly Springs, Mississippi. She was born a slave, just months before the **EMANCIPATION PROCLAMATION**. Her parents were James and Elizabeth Wells. They were slaves. After the Civil War, they continued in their professions, James as a carpenter and Elizabeth as a cook. Ida was the oldest of eight children.

IDA B. WELLS WENT TO SCHOOL at one of the first schools for blacks created in post-Civil War Mississippi. She attended Rust College in Holly Springs. It was a school for freedmen and women, and their children. Her parents both valued education highly. All the children were urged to study and to learn.

Ida loved to read. She once noted that she had read every book in the school library. But there was something missing. "I had read the Bible and Shakespeare through," she recalled. "But I had never read a Negro book or anything about Negroes."

Tragically, Ida's parents and one sibling died in a Yellow Fever epidemic in 1878. Even though she was only 16, Ida was determined to keep her family together. She spent the next several years working and raising her sisters and brothers.

FIRST JOBS: After her parents died, Wells needed a job. She convinced a nearby school official that she was 18 and was hired as a teacher. The school was six miles away, so she had to live near the school. Local relatives looked after her siblings during the week. Every weekend, Wells would make the trip home. "I came home every Friday, riding on the back of a big mule. I spent Saturday and Sunday washing and ironing and cooking for the children, and went back to my country school on Sunday afternoon."

In 1883, Wells took a teaching job near Memphis, Tennessee. She moved there with her two youngest sisters. They lived with her Aunt Fannie. Wells began to teach in Woodstock, Tennessee.

Wells still wanted to learn. In the summer, she took courses at Fisk University. That qualified her to teach in the Memphis public schools. She taught first grade in Memphis for seven years. She loved teaching, but she was appalled at the quality of her segregated school. It was the world of **JIM CROW**. Schools for black children lacked books, teaching materials, even decent buildings.

For Wells, it was part of a pattern of racial injustice she would fight all her life.

FIGHTING RACIAL DISCRIMINATION: One day, Wells was riding in the first-class compartment of a train. A conductor told her to move to the "colored car" and give up her seat to a white man. Wells had paid for a first-class ticket. She refused to move. When the conductor tried to remove her by force, she bit him. Finally, with two other men, the conductor removed Wells from the train car. The white riders in the first-class compartment cheered. Wells vowed to get justice.

Wells sued the railroad company, the Chesapeake & Ohio. At that time, there was a law, enacted in 1875, that banned racial discrimination in theaters, hotels, and public transportation. The law was largely ignored, especially in the South. But the law was on Wells's side.

Well's won her case in the local circuit courts. But the railroad company appealed the decision. The Tennessee Supreme Court reversed the lower court decision.

Wells wasn't discouraged. Instead, she decided to devote her life to fighting injustice. She decided to become a journalist to make her opinions known. Her first articles appeared in a church newspaper for blacks, *The Living Way*. She wrote about racial discrimination, especially about the plight of poor blacks. Because she criticized the lack of good schools for blacks, she was fired from her teaching job.

A CRUSADING JOURNALIST: In 1889, Wells became part-owner of a newspaper, the *Free Speech and Headlight*. She wrote about racial discrimination against blacks, often under the pen name "Iola."

In 1892, three black businessmen who were friends of Wells opened a grocery store to serve blacks. They competed for customers with the white-owned grocery store in the neighborhood. They drew away many black customers, and the white owners were angry.

One night, a white mob attacked the black grocery store. The owners fought back, and one of the attackers was shot. The three black men were taken to jail. A white mob took them from the jail and murdered them. It was a lynching.

LYNCHING: The term "lynching" means the murder of an individual, usually by a mob, and always outside of the law. The term is usually used to describe the violent murder of blacks by whites.

BECOMING AN ANTI-LYNCHING CRUSADER: The lynching of her friends inflamed Wells and the black community of Memphis. She wrote a series of scathing editorials in *The Free Speech* about the murders. Here's a sample of what she wrote:

"The city of Memphis has demonstrated that neither character nor standing avails the Negro if he dares to protect himself against the white man or become his rival. There is only one thing left to do. Save our money and leave a town which will neither protect our lives and property, nor give us a fair trial in the courts, but takes us out and murders us in cold blood when accused by white persons."

Wells's courageous words proved to be powerful. Many blacks did indeed move away from Memphis. And Wells faced personal danger. The offices of *The Free Speech* were destroyed. She received death threats.

MOVING TO CHICAGO: Wells moved to Chicago for her own safety. She continued to publish articles in *The New York Age*. She also began a systematic study of lynching. She researched the topic thoroughly. Sometimes she even investigated the lynching sites, putting herself in great personal danger.

In 1893, Wells left on a speaking tour of England. She received warm support for her crusade against lynching and for racial justice.

Wells returned to Chicago and her writing. She published a pamphlet, then a book based on her research into lynching. The book's title was *The Red Record: Tabulated Statistics and Alleged Causes of Lynchings in the United States.* In it, she exposed the truth behind lynching. She documented how white mobs lynched blacks based on false charges. Wells's research showed that black men risked death for things like not paying a debt, stealing hogs, or testifying in court.

Wells was also active in forming groups of blacks, especially women, to make their voices heard. She founded the first black women's group to fight for the right of women to vote. She joined Susan B. Anthony and other members of the women's rights movement.

FOUNDING THE NAACP: In 1909, Wells became one of the founders of the **NAACP (National Association for the Advance-**

ment of Colored People). She joined with other activists like **W. E. B. Du Bois** in founding one of the most important Civil Rights organizations in the U.S. She also opposed the policies of **Booker T. Washington**. She thought he was too accommodating to whites.

CONTINUING TO WORK FOR JUSTICE: Wells continued the fight for equality. She worked for good schools for blacks, and founded the first kindergarten for black children. She even ran for the Illinois state legislature.

IDA B. WELLS'S HOME AND FAMILY: In 1895, Wells married a Chicago lawyer named Ferdinand L. Barnett. He was the publisher of *The Conservator*. That was the first black newspaper in Chicago. After that, she became known as "Ida Wells-Barnett." They had four children, two sons and two daughters. Wells-Barnett continued to work for Civil Rights until her death on March 25, 1931. She was 69 years old.

HER LEGACY: Ida B. Wells is remembered for her fearless crusade for racial justice. In her writings against lynching, she brought the truth of racial violence to the world. Even faced with great personal danger, she showed courage and conviction. She is honored as one of the most dynamic leaders of the Civil Rights movement.

WORLD WIDE WEB SITES:

http://lcweb2.loc.gov.ammem/aap/idawells.html
http://www.duke.edu/~ldbaker/classes/AAIH/ibwells/
http://www.lkwdpl.org/wihohio/barn-ida.htm
http://www.webster.edu/~woolflm/idabwells/html

Tiger Woods
1975 -
African-American Professional Golfer
First African-American to Win the Masters Tournament

TIGER WOODS WAS BORN on December 30, 1975, in Long Beach, California. His parents were Earl and Kultida (kuhl-TEE-dah) Woods. Earl was a former U.S. Army officer. He died in 2006. Kultida, who was born in Thailand, is a homemaker. Tiger has two half-brothers, Kevin and Earl Jr., and a half-sister, Royce. They are the children from his father's first marriage.

Tiger's real first name is Eldrick. He got the nickname "Tiger" from his dad. His father fought in the Vietnam War in the 1960s and

Tiger at age eight.

had a Vietnamese friend, nicknamed "Tiger," who saved his life. He decided to give his son the nickname of his wartime friend.

TIGER WOODS GREW UP in the city of Cypress, California, near Los Angeles. Tiger started learning about golf when he was just a baby.

STARTING TO PLAY GOLF: Tiger's dad decided he wanted to try to raise the greatest golfer ever. So when Tiger was just six months old, his dad would put him in a highchair in the garage and have Tiger watch him hit balls. According to his dad, Tiger could watch for hours.

When he was only two years old, Tiger played his first round of golf. He used golf clubs that had been sawed off to fit him. He was soon playing so well that he caught the attention of the media. Soon he was appearing on TV shows, like "CBS News" and "That's Incredible."

Tiger began taking lessons with a golf pro at age four. His teacher, Rudy Duran, remembers that Tiger was unlike any kid he'd ever seen. "It was mind-boggling to see a 4½-year-old swinging like a pro," he remembered.

THE GAME OF GOLF: In golf, the object is to take the least amount of shots, called "strokes," to get from the beginning of each hole to the end. A round of golf usually includes 18 holes. Each hole is supposed to be finished in a certain number of strokes. If a golfer completes the hole in that number, he or she has gotten a "par" for that hole. The player with the least amount of strokes wins the game.

BEGINNING TO COMPETE: Tiger began to compete in golf tournaments when he was eight years old. That first year, he won the Optimist International World Junior Tournament. By the time he was 11, he'd won a string of 30 championships. People were amazed at Tiger Woods, for his golfing ability and for his attitude.

Tiger's parents made sure that he always played with good manners and good sportsmanship. Once during a tournament he made a bad shot and had a temper tantrum. His mother promptly told the tournament director to penalize her son for his behavior. Tiger calmed right down.

MAKING TIME FOR A REGULAR CHILDHOOD: Tiger's parents also made sure that he didn't just play golf. "Hey, I had a normal childhood," Tiger remembers. "I did the same things every kid did. I studied and went to the mall. I was addicted to TV wrestling, rap music, and 'The Simpsons.' I got into trouble and got out of it. I loved my parents and obeyed what they told me. The only difference is I can sometimes hit a little ball into a hole in less strokes than some other people."

TIGER WOODS WENT TO SCHOOL at the local public schools in California. His parents always stressed the importance of school, and Tiger was a good student. "School comes first, golf second," said Tiger. "How much practice I do in golf is determined by how soon I finish my homework. You can't accomplish anything without an education."

Tiger went to Orangeview Junior High and Anaheim Western High School. After graduating from high school, he went to Stanford University in California. Tiger did so well in school and golf that he won a golf scholarship to Stanford.

Tiger playing for Stanford.

COMBINING GOLF AND COLLEGE: In college Tiger studied business and kept improving his golf game. He won the U.S. Junior Amateur Tournament three years in a row, in 1991, 1992, and 1993. Then he moved up to the U.S. Amateur Tournament. He won that competition in 1994, 1995, and 1996. He also won the major college tournament, the NCAA Championship, in 1996.

In 1996, Tiger began to play in tournaments with professional golfers. Because he was such an outstanding amateur, he was invited to play in the most important golf matches in the world. In tournaments like the U.S. Open, the British Open, and the Masters, he played with golf's greatest. And those players, like Jack Nicklaus, were impressed with Tiger. "He'll win more Masters titles than Arnold Palmer and I did combined," Nicklaus predicted.

TURNING PRO: Woods decided to turn pro in 1996. He left college, but promised to return to finish his business degree later. It was a hard decision. He wanted to play with the best, and to make his living at it. As an amateur, he couldn't accept money for winning. He could as a pro.

Still, said Tiger, it was never about money. "It was about being happy. I have been thinking about this for a long time." His first income after turning pro was for endorsements. Nike payed him $40 million to advertise its products, and Titleist paid him $3 million.

But Tiger Woods didn't let the money go to his head. He started out on the pro tour in 1997 with the ability and determination of a champion.

THE 1997 MASTERS TOURNAMENT: Tiger Woods entered the record books, and the hearts of millions, for his performance at the 1997 Masters.

The Masters Tournament is one of the most important competitions in golf. It is played at Augusta National in Augusta, Georgia. The course is one of the most beautiful, and one of the most difficult, in golf.

Tiger with his mother, Kultida Woods.

Tiger Woods began his first day at the Masters with a terrific score of 70. Over the four days of the tournament, he played better than anyone ever had on the course. With the pressure of millions of TV viewers and against the best players in the game, Tiger Woods won the 1997 Masters with a record 270 strokes for three days.

He didn't show any emotion, just steely determination on hole after hole. But after he had won the tournament, he ran to his father's arms and cried.

At 21, Tiger Woods was the youngest player ever to win the Masters. He was also the first African-American or Asian ever to win the Masters or any other major tournament.

In his first five years as a pro, Woods became one of the best golfers ever. In 1999, he became the first golfer to win four consecutive PGA events since the legendary Ben Hogan. In 2001, he became the first person in history to hold all four major championships at the same time: the Masters, the PGA Championship, the U.S. Open, and the British Open. He won back-to-back Masters in 2001 and 2002. He also won the U.S. Open in 2002.

Woods had a brief setback in 2002, when he had to have knee surgery. In 2003 and 2004 he seemed to struggle. He hired a new coach, Hank Hanley. Hanley helped him regain his winning form.

The 2005 season saw Tiger back in top shape. He won six tournaments, including the Masters and the British Open. He regained his ranking as Number One in pro golf.

In 2006, Woods started out strong. He won the British Open for the third time. He also won the PGA Championship. He was named the PGA Player of the Year for the eighth time. But the year also brought him great personal sadness.

A FAMILY TRAGEDY: Tiger Woods lost his greatest mentor and friend, his dad, in May 2006. It was a great tragedy for Tiger and his family.

The 2007 season brought personal joy and professional triumph to Woods. He tied for second at the Masters. On June 18, 2007, the day before the U.S. Open, he became a dad. His wife, Elin, gave birth to their first child, a daughter named Sam Alexis. In August 2007, Woods showed how strong he still was. He won his 13th major title, the PGA Championship. Cheering him on were his wife and new baby.

Afterwards, Woods reflected on his year. "It's a feeling I've never had before, having Sam and Elin there. It feels a lot more special when you have your family there. It used to be my mom and dad. Now we have our own daughter. It's evolved, and this one feels so much more special."

As the 2007 season drew to a close, Woods was playing some of the finest golf of his life. He's won 81 tournaments to date. He's played 230 PGA tour events and won 61 of them. He won the Tour Championship in September 2007 with the lowest score of his career, 23 under par. But he's not satisfied. Afterwards, Tiger was asked if he ever expected to play any better than he is now. His answer was a resounding "Yes!"

ETHNIC HERITAGE: Tiger Woods is very proud of his background. "I am the product of two great cultures—one African-American and the other Asian. The bottom line is that I am an American . . . and proud of it!"

TIGER WOODS'S HOME AND FAMILY: Woods met Swedish model and nanny Elin Nordegren in 2001. They dated for several years and got married on October 5, 2004. On Tiger's 31st birthday in December 2006, he announced that he and Erin were expecting a baby. Their daughter, Sam Alexis Woods, was born in June, 2007. Tiger was ecstatic to be a dad. "This is truly a special time in our lives and we look forward to introducing Sam to our family and friends over the next few weeks," he said.

Woods started a charity several years ago. The Tiger Woods Foundation is dedicated to helping young people to reach their potential through community-based programs. The organization funds educational and health programs all over the country.

HIS LEGACY: It's too early to state what Tiger Woods's legacy is. He will certainly go down in history as one of the finest golfers of all time. He is also one of the most popular golfers in history. He has brought many new players, including many young African-American players, to the game. He hopes to inspire kids to do well, in sports and in school, for years to come.

Tiger hugs his father, Earl Woods.

WORLD WIDE WEB SITES:

http://sports.espn.go.com/golf/players/
http://www.pgatour.com/players/00/8/93/
http://www.tigerwoods.com
http://www.twfound.org/

Photo and Illustration Credits

Every effort has been made to trace copyright for the images used in this volume. Any omissions will be corrected in future editions.

Hank Aaron: AP Images

Muhammad Ali: AP Images; Cin America Releases, Inc.

Arthur Ashe: AP Images

Crispus Attucks: Courtesy of the Library of Congress

Benjamin Banneker: Courtesy of the Maryland Historical Society, Baltimore, Maryland

Mary McLeod Bethune: Courtesy of the Library of Congress

Jim Brown: AP Images

Ralph Bunche: Courtesy of the Library of Congress; Courtesy UN Photo

Ben Carson: Courtesy Johns Hopkins/Keith Weller Photography

George Washington Carver: Courtesy of the Library of Congress; Courtesy Iowa State University Library/University Archives

Frederick Douglass: Courtesy of the Library of Congress

W.E.B. Dubois: Courtesy of the Library of Congress

Matthew Henson: Courtesy of the Library of Congress

Jesse Jackson: Courtesy of the Library of Congress

Mae Jemison: Courtesy NASA

Lonnie Johnson: Courtesy Johnson Research & Development Co.

Michael Jordan: Newscom.com; AP Images

Jackie Joyner-Kersee: AP Images; UCLA Sports Information Dept.

Coretta Scott King: Courtesy of the Library of Congress; AP Images

Martin Luther King, Jr.: Courtesy of the Library of Congress; Courtesy of the King Center; Courtesy of LBJ Library/photo by Yoichi R. Okamoto

Malcolm X: Courtesy of the Library of Congress

Thurgood Marshall: Courtesy of the Library of Congress

Elijah McCoy: University of Southern Indiana Dept. of Engineering

Garrett Morgan: The Western Reserve Historical Society, Cleveland, Ohio

Jesse Owens: AP Images:

Leroy Paige: AP Images:

Rosa Parks: Courtesy of the Library of Congress

Colin Powell: Courtesy the U.S. State Dept.; Newscom.com.

Condolezza Rice: Courtesy of the U.S. State Dept.; National Security Council

Jackie Robinson: AP Images

Wilma Rudolph: AP Images

Bill Russell: AP Images

Sojourner Truth: Courtesy of the Library of Congress

Harriet Tubman: Courtesy of the Library of Congress

Booker T. Washington: Courtesy of the Library of Congress

Ida B. Wells: Courtesy of the Library of Congress

Tiger Woods: AP Images; Stanford University Sports Information; *Orange County Register*

Glossary
and
Brief Biographies

The Glossary contains terms used in the entries on African-American Leaders. It includes descriptions and definitions of concepts relating to African-American history and culture. The "Brief Biographies" section includes short profiles of people important to African-American history who do not have full entries in the volume. Glossary terms are capitalized and bold-faced in the entries.

ABOLITION, ABOLITIONIST: The abolitionist movement began in the 1780s in the United States and Europe. Abolitionists wanted to "abolish," or end, slavery, as well as the slave trade. In the 1830s, William Lloyd Garrison started the American Anti-Slavery Society. He called for the freeing of all slaves throughout the nation. **Frederick Douglass** was an early an ardent advocate of abolition, as were **Sojourner Truth** and **Harriet Tubman.**

BROWN V. THE BOARD OF EDUCATION: In 1954, **Thurgood Marshall** was one of the **NAACP** attorneys in a case called "Brown v. Board of Education of Topeka." (Legal cases are named for the two sides in the suit. In this case, Marshall and the NAACP represented Oliver Brown against the Topeka, Kansas, Board of Education.)

311

At that time, 17 states and the District of Columbia had laws that segregated schools. In the north, states left the decision up to individual school districts. In Topeka, Kansas, schools were legally segregated. All over the country, black children went to schools where buildings were crumbling and books were scarce. The states could *legally* spend more on white students, their teachers, and their facilities than they could for blacks.

Oliver Brown was the father of seven-year-old Linda Brown. He filed the suit on Linda's behalf. Linda had to travel 1 hour 20 minutes to get to her segregated school each day. The school was 21 blocks from her home. She had to cross a dangerous railroad yard every day to get to the bus. Linda's white neighbors walked to a whites-only school that was just 7 blocks from her home. Her father claimed that such treatment was unconstitutional.

The new Chief Justice of the Supreme Court was named Earl Warren. He listened to the Brown case as argued by Marshall. He wrote the Court's response. He agreed with Marshall's argument. He called education "perhaps the most important function of state and local government." He also wrote:

"Does segregation of children in the public schools solely on the basis of race deprive the children of the minority group of equal educational opportunity? We believe it does."

"In the field of education, the doctrine of 'separate but equal' has no place. Separated education facilities are inherently unequal."

With that decision, the Supreme Court declared segregation unconstitutional. It took many years to integrate the public schools, but the Brown decision marked the end of legal discrimination based on race. It was one of the most important decisions of the century. It led to the end of legal segregation in all public facilities.

However, the movement for the integration of the public schools had more obstacles to overcome. In the years following the Brown decision, attempts to integrate public schools met with entrenched resistance and more racial violence. As the case of **THE LITTLE ROCK NINE** indicates, it took years, and governmental intervention, to begin to implement integration.

CIVIL RIGHTS ACT: In 1964, the U.S. Congress passed legislation called the Civil Rights Act. It prohibits discrimination based on race, color, religion, or national origin in all public places, including schools, restaurants, hotels, and theaters.

CIVIL RIGHTS MOVEMENT: The term Civil Rights Movement refers to the political and social movement that began in the early 20th century to win equal rights for African-Americans. The movement was spearheaded by such leaders as **W.E.B. Du Bois, Ralph Bunche,** and **Ida B. Wells**, working with the **NAACP**. In the 1950s and 1960s, **Martin Luther King Jr.** led the movement to its greatest legislative achievement, the passage of the **CIVIL RIGHTS ACT** of 1964. That landmark law prohibited discrimination based on race, color, religion, or national origin in all public places, including schools, restaurants, hotels, and theaters. The **VOTING RIGHTS ACT** of 1965 guaranteed free access to voting for all Americans. In addition to new laws, a major Supreme Court case furthered the cause of the movement. **BROWN VS. THE BOARD OF EDUCATION** was a case brought by **Thurgood Marshall** and the **NAACP** against the public schools of Topeka, Kansas. In that landmark decision, the Court ruled that segregation in the public schools was unconstitutional.

CIVIL WAR: The Civil War began in 1861 and continued until 1865. The war was between the Northern states, which fought for the preservation of the Union and the **ABOLITION** of **SLAVERY**, and the Southern states, which wanted slavery to continue in the South and extend into the new territories of the U.S. When Abraham Lincoln was elected President in 1860, the Southern states began to secede from the Union. They formed a new country, called the Confederate States of America. On April 12, 1861, Confederate soldiers fired on Fort Sumter, a fort held by Union (Northern) troops in South Carolina. It was an act of rebellion, and the beginning of the war.

The battles of the Civil War were fought in several states, including Virginia, Mississippi, Pennsylvania, and Tennessee. Some of the fiercest and most decisive battles took place at Bull Run, Antietam, Chancellorsville, Vicksburg, and Gettysburg. All together, more than 300,000 people died in the Civil War. The war ended on April 9, 1865, when the Army of the Confederacy, under General Robert E. Lee, surrendered to General Ulysses S. Grant, head of the Union forces.

DRED SCOTT DECISION: The Dred Scott Decision was handed down by the Supreme Court in 1856. The case had been brought by Dred Scott, a slave who had been taken from a Southern to a Northern state, where slavery was banned. Scott sued for his freedom, as a citizen of a free state. The Court, led by Justice Taney, ruled that "negroes are deemed to have no rights which white men are bound to respect."

EMANCIPATION PROCLAMATION: On January 1, 1863, Lincoln issued "The Emancipation Proclamation." It said that all slaves living in Confederate states were free. Many former slaves fled to the North, where they joined the army and fought for the Union.

THE FIFTEENTH AMENDMENT: In 1870, the U.S. Congress passed the Fifteenth Amendment. It guaranteed the rights of all citizens of any race the right to vote.

THE FOURTEENTH AMENDMENT: The Fourteenth Amendment guarantees the rights of full citizenship to all Americans, regardless of race. It was passed in 1868.

JIM CROW: After the Civil War and the passage of the Thirteenth, Fourteenth and Fifteenth Amendments, black Americans thought their hard-fought, new-won rights were guaranteed. The Thirteenth Amendment banned slavery. The Fourteenth Amendment guaranteed the right of full citizenship to African-Americans. The Fifteenth Amendment guaranteed the rights of all citizens, regardless of race, to vote.

Yet the truth of the lives of black Americans was much different. Throughout the country, particularly in the South, blacks had few if any rights. Facilities were segregated by race. Education and jobs were denied them. It took the political and social powers of the **CIVIL RIGHTS MOVEMENT**, a series of court cases, especially **BROWN V. THE BOARD OF EDUCATION** as well as the passage of the **CIVIL RIGHTS ACT** to do away with the vestiges of Jim Crow and segregation.

LITTLE ROCK NINE: After the success of **BROWN V. THE BOARD OF EDUCATION**, the **NAACP** brought court cases against school districts that were slow to comply with court-ordered desegregation of their public schools. One of those districts was Little Rock.

DAISY BATES, head of the Arkansas NAACP, organized a group of nine students to integrate Little Rock's Central High School.

The nine students were Minnijean Brown, Elizabeth Eckford, Ernest Green, Thelma Mothershed, Melba Patillo, Gloria Ray, Terrence Roberts, Jefferson Thomas, and Carolotta Walls. Together, they faced an angry mob of citizens when they first tried to attend Central in September 1957. Over the course of several days, the mob became violent, and the students and their supporters were heckled, taunted, and some of them were attacked. TV newscasters broadcast the scene of racial chaos and hatred around the world. President Dwight D. Eisenhower became involved, sending U.S. paratroopers in to protect the students and enforce the desegregation agreement.

NAACP/NATIONAL ASSOCIATION FOR THE ADVANCEMENT OF COLORED PEOPLE: The National Association for the Advancement of Colored People was formed in 1909 in response to the continuing problems of racial injustice in America. Its early leaders included **W.E.B. DuBois, Ida B. Wells, Ralph Bunche,** and **Thurgood Marshall.**

PLESSY V. FERGUSON: Plessy v. Ferguson was an 1898 U.S. Supreme Court decision. It established the legal doctrine of "separate but equal" that basically made segregation the rule of law in the U.S. It officially made African-Americans second-class citizens.

SLAVERY: Slavery is when one person is able to hold or own another person against their will. The slave has no rights and is forced to do whatever work the slave master requires.

Slavery in the New World began shortly after the arrival of the European explorers in the 1500s. The explorers captured and enslaved Native American peoples. The enslavement of African blacks began in Virginia in the 1600s. Traders from Europe captured African people who lived on the west coast of Africa. Then the European traders brought the Africans as slaves to settlements along the Atlantic coast. These settlements later became the colonies of the United States.

People in the U.S. disagreed and argued over slavery from the time of the nation's founding. By the early 1800s most Northern states were enacting laws to end slavery. Some Northerners despised slavery so much that they wanted to "abolish" it, or do away with it. Those were the **"ABOLITIONISTS"** (see above).

But in the South, slaves had worked on plantations since the time of the first settlers. Slaves became especially important to raising crops on the plantations. They did much of the work that earned the money for their white owners. The system of slavery was part of life for white Southerners. Despite its inhumane treatment of black people, the South wanted to keep slavery. And they wanted to extend it.

In the 1800s, the nation was growing as new territories were added in the West. Settlers from the North and South moved into these territories. They disagreed over whether there should be slavery in those new areas. In the 1850s the U.S. Congress tried to work out compromises that would satisfy both the North and the South. The compromises didn't work.

Abraham Lincoln was elected President in 1860. He opposed slavery and wanted to abolish it. After Lincoln's election, eleven Southern states "seceded"—left—the Union. They formed their own separate country, called the Confederate States of America, or the Confederacy. That led to the Civil War, which lasted from 1861 to 1865. In 1863, President Lincoln issued the "Emancipation Proclamation," which freed the slaves (see above). Two years later, in 1865, the North won the war, and the South surrendered. The Confederate states once again became part of the United States, and all the slaves throughout the country were freed.

THE THIRTEENTH AMENDMENT: The Emancipation Proclamation had only freed blacks in the states that had seceded. In December 1865, the thirteenth amendment, which abolished slavery throughout the U.S,. became law.

UNDERGROUND RAILROAD: A secret network of roads and safe houses used by runaway slaves. Traveling at night, they escaped the South and found safety and freedom in the North. The "railroad" led all the way to northern New York, Michigan, and into Canada. **Harriet Tubman** was the most famous "conductor" of the Underground Railroad. She brought hundreds of slaves to freedom.

VOTING RIGHTS ACT: The Voting Rights Act of 1965 guaranteed free access to voting for all Americans. It ended an era when blacks, especially in the South, faced threats, intimidation, literacy tests, and other tactics in trying to register and to vote.

* * *

BRIEF BIOGRAPHIES

ABERNATHY, RALPH: Abernathy (1926-1990) was a Baptist minister and leader of the **CIVIL RIGHTS** movement. He was a close colleague of **Martin Luther King Jr**. Together, they founded the Montgomery Improvement Association and the Southern Christian Leadership Conference (SCLC). Both organizations were devoted to equal rights for African-Americans. Abernathy helped organize campaigns like the marches on Washington and Selma. After King's death, Abernathy led the SCLC.

BATES, DAISY: Bates (1914-1999) was a leader of the **CIVIL RIGHTS** movement and a journalist. She was head of the Arkansas chapter of the **NAACP** and led the fight to integrate Central High School in Little Rock, Arkansas (see entry above on the **LITTLE ROCK NINE)**. Bates and her husband published a prominent black newspaper, *The Arkansas State Press*. They used it as a platform to investigate racism and bigotry.

CHISHOLM, SHIRLEY: Chisholm (1924-2005) was a legislator and teacher who in 1968 became the first African-American woman elected to the U.S. House of Representatives. She served seven terms in Congress, from 1969 to 1983. She was known as a tireless advocate for the rights of African-Americans and women. She ran for the presidential nomination in 1972. Chisholm retired from Congress in 1982 and became a college professor.

EVERS, MEDGAR: Evers (1925-1963) was a leader of the **CIVIL RIGHTS MOVEMENT** and a recruiter for the **NAACP**. He was based in Mississippi, his home state, and led protests against discrimination and for voting rights for blacks. He was murdered in 1963 by a member of the racist Ku Klux Klan. His case became a major cause for the Civil Rights movement, as his murderer was not convicted until 1994.

GARVEY, MARCUS: Garvey (1887-1940) was a Jamaican-born leader of the movement for black nationalism and separatism. He moved to New York in 1916 and founded the Universal Negro Improvement Association to promote racial pride among blacks. He didn't believe that racial integration was possible or would lead to equality for African-Americans. Instead, he urged blacks to move back to Africa, where they would be able to build a new nation, run by and for blacks. Garvey was a popular and influential leader in the 1920s, but lost many followers after his conviction for mail fraud. He went to jail in 1925 and was deported to Jamaica in 1927.

JORDAN, BARBARA: Jordan (1936-1996) was an African-American legislator, educator, and civil rights advocate. She was the first woman to serve in the Texas legislature and the second black woman to serve in the U.S. House of Representatives. (The first was **SHIRLEY CHISHOLM**). She was a powerful speaker and renowned for her eloquence, intelligence, and deep commitment to the Constitution. She served on the Judiciary Committee that investigated President Richard Nixon during the Watergate scandal in 1974. Jordan retired from Congress in 1977 and began a distinguished teaching career at the University of Texas.

THOMAS, CLARENCE: Thomas (1948-) is the second African-American to be named to the U.S. Supreme Court. (The first was **Thurgood Marshall**.) He has served on the Court since 1991. He is a controversial figure in American politics for his conservative views. He believes that African-Americans must show as individuals what they can achieve. Further, he believes that blacks must think freely, and for themselves. "I am confident that the individual approach, not the group approach, is the better, more acceptable, more supportable, and less dangerous one."

WILKINS, ROY: Wilkins (1901-1981) was a journalist and civil rights leader who spent most of his career with the **NAACP**. In 1931, he served as its assistant executive secretary and as editor of its magazine, *The Crisis*. He later became executive director of the NAACP, helped **Thurgood Marshall** prepare the **BROWN V.**

BOARD OF EDUCATION case, and organized the March on Washington in 1963.

YOUNG, ANDREW: Young (1932-) is a legislator, diplomat, minister, and **CIVIL RIGHTS** leader. He was a colleague of **MARTIN LUTHER KING JR.** and a director of the Southern Christian Leadership Conference. Young served in the U.S. House of Representatives from 1973 to 1977. He was the U.S. Ambassador to the United Nations from 1977 to 1979, under President Jimmy Carter. He was also mayor of Atlanta from 1982 to 1989.

Subject Index

This index contains the names, occupations, and key words relating to the individuals profiled in this volume. It also includes significant historical events covered in the biographical profiles. Bold-faced type indicates the main entry on an individual.